Also by Frank Sanello

The Opium Wars:
The Addiction of One Empire and the Corruption of Another

The Knights Templar:
God's Warriors, the Devil's Bankers

Steven Spielberg:
The Man, the Movies, the Mythology

Faith and Finance in the Renaissance:
The Rise and Ruin of the Fugger Empire (forthcoming)

To Kill a King:
An Encyclopedia of Royal Murders From Ancient
Egypt to the Present (forthcoming)

Hitler's Vicar:
The Roman Catholic Priest Who Ruled Slovakia
for Nazi Germany (forthcoming)

tweakers

How **Crystal Meth** Is Ravaging **Gay America**

Frank Sanello

alyson books
los angeles

MANUFACTURED IN THE UNITED STATES OF AMERICA.

THIS TRADE PAPERBACK ORIGINAL IS PUBLISHED BY ALYSON PUBLICATIONS,
P.O. BOX 4371, LOS ANGELES, CALIFORNIA 90078-4371.
DISTRIBUTION IN THE UNITED KINGDOM BY TURNAROUND PUBLISHER
SERVICES LTD.,
UNIT 3, OLYMPIA TRADING ESTATE, COBURG ROAD, WOOD GREEN,
LONDON N22 6TZ ENGLAND.

FIRST EDITION: FEBRUARY 2005

05 06 07 08 09 **a** 10 9 8 7 6 5 4 3 2

ISBN 1-55583-884-7
ISBN-13 978-1-55583-884-3

CREDITS
COVER PHOTOGRAPHY BY DAVID JENSEN.
COVER DESIGN BY MATT SAMS.

For Cesare, Catullus, Pellegrino, and Thisbe

Contents

Acknowledgments

Many thanks to Daniel Abraham, Kyle Baker, Edith
Barcay, A. Scott Berg, Ellen Bersch, Professor Joseph
Boone, Dr. Daniel Bowers, André Brooks, Angela Brown,
Nigel Cairns, Charles Casillo, Louis Chunovic, Dr. Gary
Cohan, Carrie Cohen, Jim Chud, Hector DeJean, Ghalib
Dhalla, Michael Dorr, Anita Edson, Mike Emmerich,
Cyrus Godfrey, Lawrence C. Goldstein, Mary and Art
Goodale, André Guimond, Dr. Stephen Graham, Mike
Hamilburg, Scott Hill, Dr. Scott Hitt, Chris Hix,
Frederick Hjelm, Dr. Derek Jones, Brad Kane, Steven
Kay, Gary Kirkland, Pamela Lansden, Robert Lent,
Michael Levine, Will Litchfield, Rod Lurie, Christina
Madej, Charlie Medrano, Paul Manchester, David
Marlow, Greg Middleton, Kevin Moreton, Jim Murphy,
Tom Packard, James Robert Parish, Ross Plotkin, Dr. Dale
Prokupek, Sia Prospero, Lee Ray, Linda and Phil Reinle,
Dr. William Resnick, Ray Richmond, Doris Romeo,
Marjorie Rothstein, Sarkis, Catherine Seipp, Rob Senger,
Guy Shalem, Professor Benjamin Sifuentes-Jauregui,
Dorie Simmonds, Bryan Smith, Chris Spengler, Monica
Trascendes, Christopher Villa, Denise Wallace, Dan
Wise, Dean Wong, and Jeff Yarbrough.

Introduction

More than 250 crystal users and those who treat them were interviewed for this book. One after another, stories were told of lives destroyed by a seductive drug, the use of which typically begins on weekends or special occasions but then ends up overwhelming the user's life, relationships, and career.

When friends and acquaintances were told the subject of this book, there was often a sigh of relief followed by a statement suggesting that there is a compelling need for a book like this that will get the message out there about the destructive effects of this so-called "party" drug.

Tweakers: How Crystal Meth Is Ravaging Gay America includes case histories—of those who use and abuse crystal as well as those who have stopped using the drug and are in recovery or remission from the chronic, recurring illness of drug addiction. (Some names and/or identifying characteristics of those interviewed for this book have been changed at the interviewee's request.) Each individual interviewed knew someone—usually himself—whose life was careening out of control due to crystal. Many of these lost souls seemed to be in a classic state of denial, insisting that they had their drug usage under control. Others expressed concern that perhaps crystal was having more of an impact on their lives than they had thought it would when they first started using.

Then, there were the saddest cases, where the drug user was well aware of the mayhem that the drug was wreaking in his or her life. For these users, knowledge was not power; it only reinforced their sense of helplessness and hopelessness as they engaged in the circular phenomenon of use—binge, crash, and then use more—to alleviate the physical and psychological pain of the crash caused by withdrawal.

Tweakers also examines the 100-year history of crystal meth—also known as Tina, speed, crank, chalk, quartz, go-fast, zip, cristy, jib, ice, and glass—and the effects the drug has on the brain. Experts in the field of drug addiction offer their theories as to why crystal is so popular in the gay community—as well as suggestions for treatment. The crucial distinctions between drug use, abuse, and addiction are also explained.

Although this drug is not discriminating about whose lives it will destroy, crystal use has had a particularly devastating impact on the gay community. *Tweakers* is an attempt to get to the bottom of this destruction—while also providing hope and help to those who suffer.

—Frank Sanello

Ingredients for Making Meth

HYDROCHLORIC ACID, LEAD ACETATE, DRAIN CLEANER (DRANO), BATTERY AND POOL ACID, LYE, LITHIUM BATTERIES, LANTERN FUEL, LIQUID FERTILIZER, IODINE, LIGHTER FLUID, ANHYDROUS AMMONIA, ETHER, SODIUM CYANIDE, ACETONE, RED PHOSPHORUS, ANTIFREEZE, PSEUDOEPHEDRINE, PHENYL-PROPANOLAMINE, EPHEDRINE, AMMONIA, ETHER.

—UNCLE FESTER'S TOP-SELLING METH COOKBOOK, *THE SECRETS OF METHAMPHETAMINE MANUFACTURE*

The Other Gay Plague

"ONCE SOMEBODY GETS INTO CRYSTAL, THEY'RE JUST GOING TO GO DOWN THE TOILET."

—THOMAS NEWTON, ASSOCIATE PROFESSOR OF PSYCHIATRY AT UCLA'S NEUROPSYCHIATRIC INSTITUTE AND THE MEDICAL DIRECTOR OF UCLA'S SUBSTANCE ABUSE INPATIENT SERVICE

"ON SATURDAY NIGHTS, THE E.R. IS PACKED WITH GAY GUYS WHO ARE HAVING PROBLEMS WITH CRYSTAL AND ITS INTERACTION WITH OTHER PARTY DRUGS."

—MICHAEL MAJESKI, CLINICAL PSYCHOLOGIST

"I WOULD GIVE MY LIFE TO NEVER HAVE TRIED SPEED FOR THE FIRST TIME. PLEASE, PLEASE, PLEASE, I AM BEGGING YOU. NEVER TRY SPEED."

—JAMIE

"THERE'S A WHOLE SUBCULTURE WITHIN THE GAY SUBCULTURE THAT REVOLVES AROUND CRYSTAL."

—KEVIN KURTH, EDUCATION AND OUTREACH COORDINATOR

Michael Majeski, a clinical psychologist in West Hollywood, California, who specializes in the treatment of drug and sex addiction, wryly claims that there are two fashionable "places to be" for gay men in Los Angeles on a Saturday night: One is West Hollywood's most popular gay dance club, and the other is the emergency room at Cedars-Sinai Medical Center—conveniently located just a few miles away.

"On Saturday nights the E.R. is packed with gay guys who are having problems with crystal and its interaction with other party drugs," Majeski says. Some of the E.R. patients have binged on so much crystal that they display the symptoms of a full-blown panic attack, he says. They also have the gaunt and wasted look of AIDS patients before the advent of protease inhibitors.

Statistics bear out the anecdotal evidence that

methamphetamine use has become a nationwide health crisis. According to the National Household Survey on Drug Abuse published in 2000, almost 9 million people (4% of the population) have used methamphetamine at least once. According to KCI: The Anti-Meth Site, "No one ever tries meth just once."

The crystal crisis in the gay community is particularly acute. Orlando Rivera, a substance abuse specialist at Gay and Lesbian Adolescent Social Services (GLASS) in West Hollywood, California, says crystal use among gays has reached "epidemic proportions at this point." Tony Zimbardi—a staff psychologist at the Tarzana Treatment Center in Los Angeles's San Fernando Valley that offers services for HIV patients and alcohol and drug abusers— agrees that crystal use is "pretty much devastating [the gay] community."

"Sex and Love," a survey conducted by the Center for HIV Education Studies and Training (CHEST) at Hunter College of the City University of New York, found that out of the 2,335 gay and bisexual men interviewed in the fall of 2003 and spring of 2004, 22% had used meth and 10.4% had used it in the past three months. The study also found that the younger the man, the more likely it was that he had used recently (the study polled men ages 18 to 84).

Since so much of gay social life seems to revolve around sexual activity, Zimbardi says, it's no surprise that a drug that turbocharges sexual pleasure should prosper in that environment. "Crystal increases the libido, and sexual activity that in the past might have lasted half an hour can go on for hours on crystal," adds Mark Hufford, a drug counselor in Hollywood who is also a recovering addict. Some of the addicts interviewed for this book describe even longer marathon sexual sessions that lasted days and weeks.

Zimbardi adds that crystal is "probably the [number 1] cause of HIV transmission. We're not finding high rates of new infection among gay men who aren't crystal users." The "Sex and Love" study concurs, showing that "the HIV-positive men reported much higher rates of having used crystal (39.2% vs. 18.9%) and more recent use of crystal (20.8% vs. 9%) compared to HIV-negative men." Also, the study finds that only 22.1% of HIV-negative men said they had unprotected and receptive sex with a partner who was HIV-positive while on crystal, but 57.4% of HIV-positive men said they'd had unprotected and receptive sex with an HIV-negative partner while on crystal.

The Los Angeles Gay & Lesbian Center (LAGLC) in Hollywood hosts support groups for people living with HIV and AIDS. Joni Lavick, the center's director of mental health services, reports that "at least 50%" of the center's clients have "a substance abuse or dependency issue in addition to whatever else is bringing them in for therapy. And crystal is the drug of choice."

Neva Chauppette is a clinical psychologist in private practice who also works at the Tarzana Treatment Center. Many of Chauppette's patients are also HIV-positive; crystal, she explains, gives them the energy to compensate for chronic fatigue syndrome, a common symptom of HIV infection. The drug is also especially attractive to gay people who have internalized homophobia. "If you're conflicted about expressing yourself in a gay manner, crystal not only gives you control [over internalized homophobia], it will also erase it," says Chauppette.

The Crystal Subculture

"There's a whole subculture within the gay subculture that revolves around crystal," says Kevin Kurth, the education and outreach coordinator at Being Alive, a peer-based AIDS services organization in West Hollywood. Based on his experience leading support groups for gay men who have recently become infected with HIV, Kurth believes that a large percentage of seroconversions result from crystal use.

Cathy Reback runs the prevention division at the Van Ness Recovery House, an inpatient drug and alcohol rehabilitation facility in the Hollywood district of Los Angeles. Van Ness sends survey teams to gay bars, bathhouses, sex clubs, and circuit parties. According to Reback, the Van Ness teams have found that crystal is the number 1 drug used at circuit parties and the number 3 drug (after alcohol and marijuana) used at sex clubs and bathhouses.

Crystal has been so devastatingly successful in these social contexts largely because it is so affordable and easy to get. "It's cheap, freely available, and offers a quick and intense high," says Kevin Kurth.

The Koch Crime Institute, a Kansas-based nonprofit think tank devoted to crime prevention and reduction, reported in 1999 that although prices vary from region to region, one gram of crystal on average cost $240, although prices varied from region to region. An ounce in 1999 wholesaled for $1,700 and provided approximately 110 doses that users call "bumps." Two years later, the price of crystal had been slashed to $80 per gram. (Note: The Koch Crime Institute has since become KCI: The Anti-Meth Site, which functions as an online clearinghouse focusing on the abuse of crystal meth and other drugs.)

During congressional testimony in 2003, Rogelio Guevara, chief of operations for the U.S. Drug Enforcement Administration, said that an ounce of crystal at that time costed only $500, less than one-third of the 1999 cost of $1,700. A gram could be bought for as little as $25, a dramatic falloff from its 2001 cost of $80.

Will, an Internet marketing executive who designed the Web site for Crystal Meth Anonymous, agrees that crystal is a bargain. "It's more cost-effective than a lot of the [other] drugs in the gay community. A small amount goes a long way, which makes it appealing to guys living in expensive gay urban centers."

Cary Quashen owns and operates Action Family Counseling, a chain of residential drug treatment facilities in seven American cities. As a certified addiction specialist and drug counselor, Quashen says this about crystal: "Right now it's the drug of choice. It afflicts everyone, from gays to adolescent girls. Crystal has become an epidemic because it's cheap, lasts a long time, and brings you to a sexual peak. At least [drug users] think it does.

Indeed, a bulletin released by the FBI in 2000 said that although methamphetamine in the past had been considered a "poor man's cocaine," today's meth users come from all strata of society. "School girls are doing it," says Cary Quashen of Action Family Counseling.

For many users, cravings for crystal come in the form of surprise attacks: You never know when they're going to hit. Doug, a 45-year-old gay man in a committed relationship, writes on KCI's message board of his boyfriend's problem: "Last night during sex, right in the middle of everything, he got up and said 'I have to find some party favors,' [and] went to the phone and started making calls." After driving him around until 4 A.M., Doug told him they had to leave because he had to be at work in three hours, only to get a response of "Leave me here, I'm frustrated and confused, so I need to walk the streets." Doug adds, "This kind and sweet man is hooked on this awful drug, and I am at a loss as to what to do for him. He is wealthy, lives in a beautiful downtown condo, has a great job, and I am filled with worry about what will become of him. How on earth is this happening here in this great land of ours?"

Are You a Tweaker?

If you use crystal and wonder if it is impacting your life in a negative way, consider the following, provided by the Atlanta branch of Crystal Meth Anonymous:

> *It doesn't matter what you call it. It doesn't matter how you did it. It brought us to our knees, because of, without exception, what it does.*
>
> *Is crystal a problem in your life? Are you an addict? Only you can answer those questions. For most of us who have admitted defeat, the answer is very clear. Yes, we had a problem with crystal, and no, we couldn't fix the problem by ourselves. We had to admit defeat to win. Crystal was our master.*
>
> *We couldn't control our drug use. What started out as weekend or occasional use became daily use, and we soon found ourselves beyond human aid. We truly suffered from a lack of power to fix our problem.*
>
> *Some of us used speed as a tool to work harder and longer, but we couldn't keep a job. Others picked at their faces and arms for hours and hours or pulled out*

their hair. Some of us had uncontrollable sexual desire. Others endlessly tinkered with projects, accomplishing nothing, but found themselves so busy they couldn't get to work on time.

We deluded ourselves into thinking that staying up for nights on end was OK, that our tweaking was under control, and that we could quit if we wanted to, or that we couldn't afford to quit, or that our using didn't affect our lives.

Maybe we saw a friend go to jail or lose his apartment, or lose his job or lose the trust of his family…or die, but our clouded minds wouldn't admit we were next. Most of us saw no way out, believing that we would use until the day we died.

Almost universally, if we had an honest moment, we found that our drug use made seemingly insurmountable problems in our lives.

The only way out was if we had the courage to admit that crystal, our onetime friend, was killing us.

It doesn't matter how you got here. The courts sent some of us; others came for family or friends; and some of us came to Crystal Meth Anonymous on our own. The question is do you want help, and are you willing to go to any lengths to change your life?

-2-

Case Histories From Hell

"I WAS ALWAYS SUCCESSFUL AT ANYTHING I
DID: ACADEMICALLY, CERTAINLY CAREER-
WISE. I WAS ALWAYS SOMEBODY WHO
ACHIEVED, AND ALWAYS THE YOUNGEST ONE
TO ACHIEVE IT. THAT WAS THE ROLE I
PLAYED IN LIFE. NOW I'M MOPPING UP
COME AT A SEX CLUB."

—MIKE

"IF YOU LOOK AT MY RÉSUMÉ YOU WOULD
NEVER SUSPECT ME AS A METH ADDICT. I
USED TO WORK OUT FIVE DAYS A WEEK AND
WAS GOING TO COMPETE IN A BODYBUILDING
SHOW. I USED TO WEIGH 245 POUNDS OF
SOLID MUSCLE.... MY ROCK BOTTOM WAS
BEING HOMELESS AND IN JAIL."

—JOSHUA

"MY BOYFRIEND, THIS KIND AND SWEET
MAN, IS HOOKED ON THIS AWFUL DRUG,
AND I AM AT A LOSS AS TO WHAT TO DO FOR
HIM. HE IS WEALTHY, LIVES IN A BEAUTIFUL
DOWNTOWN CONDO, HAS A GREAT JOB, AND
I AM FILLED WITH WORRY ABOUT WHAT
WILL BECOME OF HIM. HOW ON EARTH IS
THIS HAPPENING HERE IN THIS GREAT LAND
OF OURS?"

—DOUG

There comes a time in the lives of many alcoholics and drug addicts when a nightmarish experience while under the influence finally makes them see their substance abuse for what it is. Alcoholics Anonymous calls this "hitting bottom." KCI posts heartbreaking letters online from both users and their loved ones—case histories of people who have hit deep and desperate bottoms due to drug use.

Until a year before his posting, one KCI message board writer had no doubts about his rosy future. "I was raised by loving parents," Jamie writes. "I was given more attention, respect, understanding, and just plain love than I could ever ask for. I've never experienced a psychologically traumatizing event or suffered the death of anyone close to me."

Jamie was an exemplary student. In his junior year in high school, he made it to the finals in a statewide science competition. The next year, he earned a high score of 750 on the verbal portion of the SATs, which placed him in the top percentage of students who took the test.

He began smoking marijuana every day in his sophomore year, but the drug did not affect his scholastic achievements or work. "Even when I was smoking weed every day I got good grades, held a job, and never let it disrupt my life." During his senior year, he graduated to psilocybin (hallucinogenic "magic" mushrooms), cocaine, and Ecstasy, which he sold to classmates.

Like marijuana, none of these harder drugs impacted his life in a negative way. "Even when I was doing E [Ecstasy] and 'shrooms' [psilocybin] and coke for fun, even when I quit my job to sell E full-time, even when I became the supplier for local dealers, I still kept my shit together!"

Jamie remembers the irony of his high school graduation ceremony, when his teachers and the principal congratulated him on his academic success. "I remember shaking their hands and thinking, 'These hands have given hundreds of pills of Ecstasy to your students, and you have no fucking clue!'"

While these drugs allowed him to be what 12-step programs call a "functioning drug addict," Jamie met his match when he began using crystal. "All my knowledge, all my friends, all my family members and everyone who loves me, all my money, all my sanity—even my will to live—I traded it all for meth."

Jamie adds that he deliberately broke the hearts of everyone who ever loved him after he began using crystal. He broke more than the heart of one close friend, whom he beat so severely that the victim ended up in the hospital with a skull fracture and permanent hearing loss. He also blew thousands of dollars loaned to him on crystal. He confesses that he lied to everyone he knows: "I've betrayed most of them."

Now, at the age of 18, Jamie says he has no money, and the only clothes he has are the ones he's been wearing for the past two weeks. Jamie doesn't provide details or an explanation of how he reached this nadir, but he is forthcoming about the results of his drug use. "Totally uninvolved, innocent, oblivious people now have prices on their heads because of my stupidity," he writes. A hit man, he adds, has taken possession of his house, his family's house, and the homes of friends.

Jamie says he never saw a gun until four days ago, but in that short time both he and a friend had been shot at. Jamie doesn't say why. "I'm a pretty white boy. I had never been in a fight in my life!" he says, obviously not considering beating his friend a "fight."

Jamie accepts his responsibility for the havoc he has created. "I am absolutely, entirely, 100% responsible for the situation I'm in right now. My self-destruction was my own doing." But, he adds, if it hadn't been for crystal, "I wouldn't have taken my friends and family down with me."

Jamie's life is filled with regret and a powerful wish. "I would give my life to never have tried speed for the first time. Please, please, please. I am *begging* you. Never try speed."

Drug counselor Cary Quashen says guilt and regrets make getting sober especially difficult. "Drugs make good people feel terrible. The hardest thing about withdrawal is that they've done terrible things while using, and they hate what they have become." He says his seven residential treatment centers throughout the country "teach [drug users] to forgive themselves for what they've done."

Hitting Too Close to Home

In 1999, the National Institute of Justice examined meth users in the five Western cities of Portland, Phoenix, Los Angeles, San Diego, and San Jose and concluded that, because meth addicts amounted to only 16% of the violent crime arrests, they were less likely to be charged with a violent offense than other drug arrestees. Still, in 1997 there were 447 reported meth-related domestic incidents in Contra Costa County near San Francisco. Family members of meth addicts concur that this is definitely a rage-inducing drug.

"My brother is on meth bad," writes a concerned visitor named Jack on the KCI message board. Although crystal has caused his brother to have a stroke that paralyzed his left side, "that hasn't stopped him from doing this drug"— or from terrorizing loved ones. Jack's brother's behavior while on crystal has become threatening and extremely violent. During a meth binge, he threatened to cut off the heads of Jack's two children, aged 4 and 5, "and play basketball with them." Jack's brother also said he wanted to "slice" his mother's neck "just to watch her bleed."

"An addiction to methamphetamines dissolves one's life and ultimately causes dysfunction in ordinary day-to-day living," M. Baughman, a 2001 graduate of Narconon's rehab program, writes on MethAbuse.net. "Of course, these are only the effects the user will face. In addition, the families, children and close friends of the methamphetamine addict are also heavily affected."

Neva Chauppette adds that in her experience, "With the exception of alcohol, crystal use, more than any other drug, involves violence, domestic violence, and child abuse. You become irritable, short-fused. You misperceive people's actions or intentions, which you interpret as a threat."

Josh is another individual who has been profoundly affected by a family member's meth addition. He still starts to cry whenever he tries to talk about his brother's suicide over two years ago. So he decided to pour out his grief on the KCI message board.

On the morning of June 23, 2002, Josh woke up and went downstairs in search of his brother, who had fallen asleep on a couch in the living room the night before. But his brother was nowhere to be seen. Josh finally checked his brother's room. There he found his brother hanging dead from his belt.

Josh's brother did crystal and drank alcohol and smoked marijuana in excess. The depression that climaxed with his suicide began when Josh's brother went into debt and began borrowing money to pay for his drug habit. When Josh failed to repay these loans in a timely manner, the people who had loaned him the money "were pissed and started looking for him," Josh says. His creditors were an impatient lot who would come over at 3 A.M. and shine flashlights into the home Josh shared with his brother, finally pushing him over the edge. The tragic irony of the situation is that Josh's brother only owed his creditors $2,000—$2,000 for a human life.

From Talent Shark to Mop Jockey

Mike, 28, hasn't destroyed himself yet, but he's seen his career crash and burn. Formerly an attorney at a prominent talent agency in Beverly Hills, these days Mike can be found swabbing the sticky floors at a Los Angeles sex club. "I'm trying not to do [crystal] as much. The most I ever did it was once a week. Now it's only every couple of months," Mike says.

When he was a weekly user, Mike would only snort crystal on the weekends, then show up for work on Monday strung out and unable to function. Soon, his drug hangover ran into Tuesday, then Wednesday, until finally the entire work week was dominated by the pain and discomfort of withdrawal.

"Things that used to make me happy—lifting weights, friendships, my career—were all suffering," Mike says. "Sometimes I spent five days recovering from the weekend"—at which point it was the weekend again and time to resume his habit.

Mike says he lost his job "if not entirely because of crystal use, at least partially so." After so much slacking at the entertainment firm where high performance was the norm, Mike got called into his boss' office. His employer screamed at him, then suddenly stopped and asked, "You just don't care what I'm saying, do you?"

Mike knew his boss was right. The lawyer-turned-janitor says ruefully, "I was an overachiever before crystal. I scored in the top 1% on my SATs."

Despite the implosion of his impressive career, Mike is still in denial. Working at the sex club, he says, "has allowed me to move closer to what I really wanted to do. I needed time away from the entertainment industry. I'm really much happier now." Mike's attitude perhaps illustrates a point made by the National Institute on Drug Abuse (NIDA), a division of the National Institutes of Health: "Heavy users [of crystal] also show progressive social and occupational deterioration."

Cynthia Rushefsky, an assistant prosecutor in Greene County, Missouri, says that crystal used to be a "lower-class white drug. Now it's cutting across all socioeconomic lines. We are finding upper-middle-class, managerial types whose weekend recreational drug use has turned into addiction."

Lowest of the Low

"He was one of my lower companions," says Richard, 48, a well-known TV actor, about his hustler boyfriend. His statement sums up how some alcoholics and drug addicts like to associate with people of lower socioeconomic status when they drink or use drugs. CrystalRecovery.com puts it bluntly: "Meth users may hang out with other people whom they [normally] wouldn't go near."

In a similar vein, Los Angeles psychologist Tony Zimbardi notes, "There are two very distinct populations that crystal brings together, two different socioeconomic classes: the poor on disability and, at the other end of the economic spectrum, people with lots of disposable income and good jobs who are not yet devastated by the drug. These are two groups that don't normally cross paths."

By the time addicts finally end up in treatment with Zimbardi, class distinctions have for the most part disappeared. "I treat a lot of people, usually after they've lost everything," says Zimbardi. "That's why they seek help. They saw all the warning signs, but didn't do anything about it."

Some of Zimbardi's patients are still using drugs, and despite therapy, still don't realize they have a drug problem. "They come in every week and tell me horror stories about how they spent an entire night taking apart their car...or at a bathhouse where they had sex with six different people and didn't use a condom."

Colorado resident Duane Chapman has seen crystal

use explode from his unusual vantage point as a bounty hunter. Duane says that ""speed use was negligible" when he left Colorado and moved to Hawaii in 1991. But once he returned to Colorado in 1997, crystal use had become pandemic there. These days, 60% of Duane's work as a bounty hunter involves tracking down crystal users who have jumped bail because they're too addled by drug use to show up in court. Says Duane: "They've stayed up for three or four days or more, don't know what time it is, and miss their court dates."

Although Duane's a tough guy—he's a bounty hunter, after all—he says meth users scare him. "Users carry guns out of paranoia." He's not impressed with their personal hygiene either. "They smell from not taking showers for days at a time and live in trash-filled houses and apartments."

White-Knuckle Sobriety

Gene, 34, lives in suburban Washington, D.C. He has been clean and sober for three years, but his sobriety is the kind 12-step groups call "white-knuckle sobriety"— abstinence from drugs without the help of therapy or a 12-step program.

Crystal made Gene lose nearly everything he owned— his job, his car, his home, his confidence, and a "fair amount of dignity." His descent into homelessness, joblessness, and attempted suicide began when he was laid off from his job as an Amtrak attendant. But despite the drug's obliterating effect on his life and career, Gene still thinks about using all the time.

At the height (or depth) of his drug use, Gene was injecting himself with one eighth of a gram about every 10 hours—"sometimes more," he admits. His drug habit was costing him about $300 a week. Gene was such a loyal buyer that his dealer charged him the wholesale rate, if he got charged at all. "I would often get a little extra for being a good customer and referring friends to my dealer," Gene says. "It's a lot cheaper wholesale. If I spent $650, it would last an entire month, and I would have some to share."

Gene became homeless after an argument with his alcoholic roommate. "He had his own demons to deal with," Gene says. "We got into an argument, and I decided to leave. Plus, I was two months behind in the rent, I had already lost my job, and my car had been repossessed." After he moved out, Gene "spent a lot of time in bath-houses and all-night porn theaters."

When the economy recovered, Gene was offered his old job back, but he had to pass up the offer since the work-reentry process included random drug tests. Friends then persuaded him to check into a clinic, but in rehab Gene refused to follow the 12 steps of Alcoholics Anonymous. "I hate 12-step meetings," Gene says. "The last thing I want to do is be in a roomful of people reliving the worst moments of their lives. I really don't need to hear that every few days. I also found that people who go to meetings regularly simply traded a life-threatening behavior for an annoying habit."

People who attend 12-step meetings, Gene insists, "are shells of the people that they used to be. I don't know how many people I've seen go from fun, self-confident people to total wimps without the ability to think for themselves."

Regarding his time in rehab, Gene says, "I just needed a place to stay and get back on my feet. The rest I could do on my own." But what he thought would be an abbreviated stay turned into something much more when he was admitted to a psychiatric ward after several suicide attempts, including hanging, drug overdoses, and standing on a ledge outside a building.

Meanwhile, despite three years of sobriety, Gene says he thinks about using crystal every day—"sometimes *all* day." At the time of his interview he admitted that if he had some crystal he would use it. "I don't even have to think about that one. It's in my head. No matter what I do, I can't shake the feeling of wanting to get high...get high and have nasty sex!"

Gene's obsession with crystal suggests that he's still standing on a ledge of sorts, but he insists that he is "kind of glad" about his sobriety: "Glad I don't hear the voices anymore. Glad I have a place to live. Glad I haven't killed anyone from getting them too high."

During a second interview a few weeks after the first one, Gene was asked if he had resumed using crystal. "No, and it's not by choice either," he says. Apparently, Gene's obsession with using had turned to action: "If I had access to crystal, I probably would have done some. In fact, I have my local dealer looking for it now."

Gene was recently diagnosed as bipolar, or manic-depressive, and he's on lithium now. He says being bipolar made him use crystal. Lithium, he says, "has changed me in many ways. I don't think I would ever have taken crystal, had I been on lithium. But I did like the way crystal made me feel, and if I do it again, it will be to chase that feeling."

Bloody Hell

Andrew, a 38-year-old best-selling author and journalist, internalized so completely the stereotype of a druggie as someone who's down and out and on the streets that he remained in denial about his addiction until he hit bottom—the deepest bottom of anyone interviewed for this book.

Andrew's father had been a vicious drunk. Because Andrew knew that alcoholism is often a hereditary disease, he never drank. Although there was no history of drug addiction in his family, Andrew had also abstained from illicit drugs until about seven years ago.

It was a difficult time in Andrew's life. He had just had a "messy breakup" with his lover of 10 years. "I was in so much pain," he recalls. He then decided to anesthetize himself with crystal.

The toxic connection between drugs and sex was firmly established the first time Andrew did crystal. "I spent two days snorting with a hot guy!" he says. Andrew had snorted crystal with a psychiatrist on a phone sex line. One day he went to the doctor's place, where another guest was already trussed up in a sling, ready to shoot up.

He's a trained medical professional; he must know what he's doing, Andrew thought, so he let the doctor shoot him up. "I was already high enough and in a self-punishment mode, and the doctor was a professional, so I figured he would know the right amount"—the right amount of crystal for a mere novice like Andrew.

That was the beginning of the end. Andrew hit bottom three times, and he went into rehab in 1999, 2000, and 2001. Typically enough, each bottom was deeper than the previous one. "I was able to fool myself that it was only a weekend thing," Andrew says about his relapses. His "weekend use" soon spilled over into Monday, when he would need a snort or an injection in order to alleviate his hangover and return to work. Then, on Thursday he would tell himself, "It's almost Friday." Soon enough Andrew's weekends were starting on Thursday and ending on Monday.

In May 2002, Andrew hit what he hopes was his last bottom. It certainly was his deepest. He had only been out of rehab for eight days when he found himself, practically on autopilot, returning to his drug dealer's apartment. There the dealer injected both Andrew and himself with crystal.

What neither man knew was that other customers had broken into the dealer's apartment and cut the supply with strychnine. The customers' plan, Andrew later pieced together, was to get the dealer so sick and disoriented from the poison that they could steal his huge supply of drugs.

Andrew returned home and spent the next three days in hell. The strychnine made him go into what doctors later told him was shock. He was vomiting blood and had severe diarrhea. But Andrew didn't seek help for three days because of his fear that his friends would all abandon him if they discovered his condition; they'd said to him in the past, "If you slip again, we're going to drop you." (In 12-step parlance "slip" means relapse.) Andrew's alleged friends must have been unfamiliar with the 12-step doctrine that relapse is part of recovery.

When the paramedics finally arrived—Andrew is unclear how they got there or who called them—one of the paramedics said his apartment looked like a crime scene. "There was blood all over the place. I had vomited and bled on every towel I owned." Andrew was too sick to get dressed, so when the paramedics arrived they found him nude. He didn't have the energy to pull up his pants, so he was transported to the emergency room wearing a robe. "One of the other paramedics said 'What a loser' when he saw me nude," Andrew says.

Andrew spent the next 24 hours in the E.R., where a blood transfusion replaced his strychnine-poisoned blood. The transfusion represented a case of the cure being almost as bad as the disease. Andrew's veins had all collapsed and his arms were covered with abscesses from repeated injections (and injection attempts), so the E.R. staff ended up inserting the syringe for the transfusion into Andrew's jugular vein.

After his last admission to rehab, Andrew attended CMA meetings and forced himself to stay clean and sober; he managed to do this in part by writing one of his five published books on the entertainment industry. Although he's been in and out of rehab and 12-step programs for more than seven years, Andrew only had 15 months of sobriety at the time of the interview.

After his most recent release from rehab, Andrew abstained from sex for seven months, fearing that it would trigger the desire to use crystal. When he finally had sex again, he discovered what so many other recovering alcoholics and addicts know: Sex is better when you are clearheaded. "My libido is through the roof," Andrew says. "I come three to five times a day!"

"First, You Have to Die"

Bobby had good reason to quit. One weekend, after snorting half a gram of crystal, the 35-year-old West Hollywood resident began to hallucinate. To call his experience a "bad trip" would be an understatement.

During his lost weekend, Bobby heard voices coming from the roof of his apartment. "It sounded like somebody was being raped," he says. When he climbed up to the roof to investigate, instead of rape he saw Satan.

"I saw this real handsome spirit named Brandon, who was with a woman named Valerie. Brandon said, 'Would you like to meet the devil?' I said, 'You mean a statue of the devil?' Brandon said, 'No, it's really the devil.'

"I said, 'OK, what do I have to do?' and Brandon said, 'First, you have to die.'"

Bobby then imagined that he had died and the devil appeared to him. "He was 8 or 10 feet tall, green, his hair combed back. He wore a gray robe. He wasn't ugly, but he wasn't handsome like Brandon. The devil looked like Dracula, but he was more mischievous than evil-looking."

Still, he kept using—and the satanic hallucinations kept coming. During another binge, he imagined that devil worshippers were chasing him in an effort to sacrifice him to their master. "I could see them through the peephole of my apartment door. One guy said, 'I'm going to kill you.' But when I opened the door, nobody was there." When the TV starting talking to him, Bobby recalls that he felt like the crystal was destroying his mind.

Bobby has been in and out of Alcoholics Anonymous for years. He grew up attending Alanon meetings (a support group for relatives and friends of alcoholics) in order to deal with his stepfather, who was an alcoholic.

Bobby had been drug-free for only two weeks at the time of this interview. "Maybe I'm in denial, but I don't think crystal is addictive for me. It's more like habit-forming. I don't really crave it. Just like cocaine or booze, I can take it or leave it."

According to NIDA, with most drugs "psychotic symptoms can sometimes persist for months or years after use has ceased." Unfortunately, Bobby didn't last long enough to determine if NIDA's statement was true.

Bobby was interviewed for this book after he responded to a notice the author had posted on the bulletin board at a neighborhood gym. Six months later a notice for Bobby's funeral appeared on that same board. The note did not mention the cause of death.

-3-
This Is Your Brain on Crystal

"CRYSTAL CHANGES THE ARCHITECTURE OF THE BRAIN."
— EDWIN BAYRD, EXECUTIVE DIRECTOR OF THE UCLA AIDS INSTITUTE

"METH EATS HOLES IN YOUR BRAIN, EATS AWAY AT YOUR BONES, AND KILLS YOU AND YOUR FAMILY."
— FAWN

"TRYING METH FOR THE FIRST TIME IS LIKE TRADING YOUR BRAIN AND ENTIRE BODY AND ALL YOU HAVE TO LIVE FOR, ALL YOUR DREAMS AND DESIRES...TRADING IT FOR A QUICK ADDICTION THAT WILL PUT YOU IN JAIL, HOSPITAL, OR A REHAB WITHIN THE NEXT FIVE YEARS."
— MARIA

The brain's natural reward system governs basic needs and drives like hunger, sex, and thirst. When those needs are naturally satisfied, the brain rewards its owner with a small dose of pleasure-inducing neurochemicals such as dopamine. Crystal—tricky drug that it is—artificially rewards the user's brain by releasing torrents of dopamine and other neurotransmitters. Both the initial rush and the prolonged high from crystal occur from this sleight-of-hand stimulation of the brain.

But this gusher of dopamine short-circuits the body's natural survival instincts. According to Neva Chauppette, the brain's hunger, sleep, and thirst centers shut down because of the increased amount of dopamine in the brain while an individual is using crystal.

Crystal is dopamine's evil twin. Both drugs have a similar molecular structure. Dopamine affects the brain and spinal cord by interfering with the normal release of neu-rotransmitters, which are chemical substances used for communication between nerve cells. Dopamine is the main neurotransmitter methamphetamine acts on, and it's part of the brain's natural reward system. When you feel good about a job well done, derive gratification from fami-ly or social relationships, experience an overall feeling of contentment or believe that your life has meaning, dopamine is the neurochemical that creates these positive feelings.

According to Recovery.com the dopamine that crystal produces is equivalent to 600 times the normal amount of dopamine the brain releases in response to pleasurable events. Because of the intensity of the dopamine high brought on by crystal, it makes sense that chronic users rely more on meth for emotional rewards and less on natu-ral sources of happiness in everyday life. The National Institute on Drug Abuse describes the net effect as "decreased interest in other aspects of life, while reliance and interest in meth [as a source of pleasure] increases." NIDA cites the famous experiment in which lab animals received a dose of methamphetamine every time they pushed a lever. The animals ignored eating, drinking, and sex and ultimately died of starvation even though food and water bowls were within reach.

Meth 101

In a 1999 report, *The American Journal of Drug and Alcohol Abuse* said that methamphetamine may be swal-lowed, snorted, smoked, or injected. Smoking and injecting had the same effect, promoting the drug's rapid absorption in the lungs—which creates "immediate euphoria."

A user will continue to ingest crystal until he can't get high anymore, then crash and fall into a fitful slumber that can last several days or more. The longer the binge, the longer the crash. CrystalRecovery.com describes how addicts, after being awake for several days, will begin to "sketch" or "tweak" until they crash. Sketching or tweaking causes the drug user to become agitated, nervous, moody, irritable, and aggressive. During this stage of drug intake, the user finds it impossible to recapture the original high but hasn't crashed yet. "Nothing they do will take away the emptiness the binge has created." To smooth out the crash, users may attempt to come down by drinking alcohol, injecting heroin, or using an illicit sedative like GHB.

Injecting heroin or other dangerous substances to smooth out a crash isn't a stretch for addicts who use crystal intravenously. CrystalRecovery.com says IV meth users tend to have previously injected cocaine or heroin. In fact, according to Orlando Rivera, methamphetamine is more physically addictive than heroin. UCLA AIDS Institute's Edwin Bayrd agrees: "It may be as addictive as anything you can get your hands on."

Addicts who binge often experience a dramatic weight loss, which makes the drug popular in a culture that celebrates wafer-thin fashion models, but the downside of weight loss is that the user also becomes malnourished. Crystal suppresses appetite, but when drug intake stops, the user often experiences a rebound effect of increased appetite. The accompanying weight gain is one of the many reasons recovering crystal addicts relapse.

Still, despite its potential for abuse, methamphetamine is legally prescribed for obesity, attention-deficit hyperactivity disorder (ADHD), and narcolepsy (the inability to remain awake) under the brand name Desoxyn. It's also used as a local anesthetic for eye, ear, and throat surgeries. Because of the dangers associated with the drug, the U.S. Drug Enforcement Administration has classified crystal as a Schedule II stimulant, which means a doctor has to write a triplicate prescription, with one copy of the prescription going to the DEA, which searches for patterns of abuse in the form of illegal prescriptions for recreational rather than medical use.

The Honeymoon

Besides great sex, another reason for meth's popularity is that users who smoke or inject the drug first experience a blast of euphoria—the "rush"—which lasts only a few minutes. That state is followed by a powerful sense of well-being that can last up to eight hours. Users say the drug makes them focus better, although the ability to concentrate occurs only on the way up. An often-debilitating inability to concentrate accompanies the user on the way down.

As the drug wears off, the user "crashes" and can become anxious, depressed, and incapable of accomplishing tasks. One of the many reasons crystal is so alluring is that the user is always trying to recapture the original rush. Opium addicts in 19th-century China used to call this phenomenon "chasing the dragon." It's a feckless pursuit, a classic wild goose chase. Chasing the dragon often spurs the user to binge on the drug in an attempt to re-experience the euphoria of the first time.

"The last month of my using, I never got high, but I continued to use crystal and continued to feel the depression and angst that is associated with withdrawal," says Los Angeles drug counselor Mark Hufford. "It was very bad." Mark's friends never complained about his drug use because they were all drug users themselves. "Everyone I associated with did crystal as well, so nobody suggested I stop," says Mark. "My life became so painful, I just couldn't continue to live the way I lived. Crystal was affecting me psychologically, and I was just miserable. I stopped because I didn't want to continue the way I was living. It was a living hell."

CrystalRecovery.com notes that methamphetamine gives users almost "immediate pleasure." The subconscious remembers the initial high and tries to recapture it with repeated use. The reason users never seem able to catch the first high is that the meth-induced release of dopamine and other pleasure-stimulating neurotransmitters shuts down the brain's natural production of neurotransmitters.

Dopamine governs the body's natural reward system. MethAbuse.net describes how individuals whose natural reward systems are compromised can become "less responsive to real-life stimulators, like getting a new job, a new promotion, having lasting relationships, and in general functioning at a normal level." When the addict stops using crystal, he or she is "completely deprived of the body's natural feel-good reward system, and the addict feels an acute apathy or life-is-not-worth-living attitude." This explains why "most people who attempt to recover without effective and reliable treatment are prone to consistent relapse."

The user compensates for the depletion of neurotransmitters by using more crystal to restimulate the artificial production of dopamine. The Web site for Solutions for Recovery, a drug rehabilitation center in Dana Point, California, offers a lucid explanation of why withdrawal from crystal is so painful and relapses are so common. "As more of the methamphetamine comes into the body, more of the body's [dopamine production] is suppressed. Eventually, [dopamine production] is almost shut down completely. If the drug is removed at this time, there will be a feeling of panic. This extreme state of irritability, tension, and anxiety is what is called withdrawal."

Hannah, a novice crystal user, perfectly describes meth's honeymoon phase. In a posting on KCI's message board, she says she just used crystal for the first time, and she's still flying: "The buzz that you get off meth is so strong, so powerful. I haven't slept in two days, because all I've been doing is smoking crystal." The intense sense of pleasure brought on by the drug scares Hannah because she's read other KCI postings that describe the drug's destructive power. "I feel like this is the first stage of a battle that I'm going to lose," she writes. "All I can think is that I want more. I almost need it. That's why I'm not going to let myself have it—no matter what the cost is."

Speed Bumps

Crystal can also be ingested rectally, which is known as taking a "booty bump." Clinical psychologist and drug treatment specialist Neva Chauppette says that booty bumps represent a classic sign of addiction: the drug is inserted in the part of the body "where you want the desired effect. When administered rectally, it anesthetizes the lining of the rectum, so the pain [of anal intercourse] is reduced and protracted encounters are the norm." The anesthetic effect of crystal on rectal tissue supports NIDA's findings that "methamphetamine seems to be associated with rougher sex, which may lead to bleeding and abrasions."

"Booty bumps are a direct line to the bloodstream,"

says Mel, a 38-year-old waiter-actor living with AIDS in West Hollywood, California. "It's as powerful as injecting crystal. The quickest way to get your 'medication' short of a needle is by shoving it up your butt."

Nathan, an accountant in Redondo Beach, California, almost overdosed when a sex partner shoved a huge amount of crystal up his rectum. Unable to sleep for five days after the booty bump, Nathan hallucinated and couldn't stop shaking. "I realized I wasn't the man I wanted to be," he says. "That realization turned me around."

After hitting bottom, Nathan accumulated five years of continuous sobriety until he relapsed—and resumed using crystal, although he doesn't count it as such. "I didn't slip. I had to use medical marijuana because I have full-blown AIDS. Marijuana made me not feel sober anymore, so I drank and did crystal." Nathan thought he was going to die. "Maintaining my sobriety was not an option." He also attributes his relapse to the painkillers and all the other drugs, legal and illegal, he was using.

Regardless of the way crystal is transported into the body, for every high there's an even more dramatic low, which fosters a binge-crash-binge pattern of behavior. As euphoria turns into dysphoria, to regain the original high and forestall the painful crash, users try to retain or regain the high by repeated use of the drug.

Amphetamines on Steroids

Methamphetamine is like its molecular cousin, amphetamine, on steroids: It has a more powerful effect on the central nervous system than its parent drug. Both amphetamine and methamphetamine cause heightened, often purposeless or ineffective activity. Both drugs also suppress appetite—a popular symptom among circuit par-tygoers. On the user's way up, crystal lessens fatigue—which allows circuit party participants to stay up for events that can last all night into the early morning hours.

Meth can also result in hyperthermia (a dramatic and potentially fatal rise in body temperature, with some users reaching a temperature as high as 108 degrees), rapid breathing, irritability, insomnia, confusion, athetosis (writhing, jerky or flailing movements), extreme nervous-ness, nonstop talking, severe anorexia due to loss of appetite, tremors, convulsions, anxiety, paranoia, and aggressiveness.

In addition to elevating blood pressure, the drug also causes irregular heartbeat and can permanently damage blood vessels in the brain, causing strokes. Long-term use can lead to inflammation of the lining of the heart. The drug can also cause fatal cardiovascular collapse.

IV crystal users may damage their blood vessels to the point of collapse, and when they fail to find a plump vein to inject, they sometimes end up accidentally injecting the drug subcutaneously (under the skin), causing embarrassing abscesses. Mark Hufford says he had "abscesses on many parts of my body" after failing to locate a vein and injecting crystal subcutaneously. "I never smoked crystal. I thought it was a waste of crystal, and I never could get high that way."

Even small amounts of the drug can cause the cardio-vascular problems listed above. Less serious side effects include pupil dilation, dizziness, teeth grinding, impaired speech, dry or itchy skin, acne, numbness, and sweating.

Parkinson's Lite

Not only does crystal mimic the symptoms of mental illness, but the drug can also cause very real neurological damage. PET scans of chronic users show that "crystal changes the architecture of the brain," according to Edwin Bayrd, executive director of the UCLA AIDS Institute.

Thomas Newton, an associate professor of psychiatry at UCLA's Neuropsychiatric Institute and the medical director of the inpatient care program at UCLA's Substance Abuse Services, cites PET-scan studies that focused on the striatum, the part of the brain with which crystal binds. The striatum of crystal users showed the same damage that Parkinson's disease causes—only less dramatically. "The brain degenerates with Parkinson's," Dr. Newton says. "Parkinson's causes an 80% decline in the part of the brain that is associated with people's ability to plan and remember and feel joy. Crystal causes a decline of 25% in the same area of the brain."

Parkinson's is a severe movement disorder that has afflicted, among others, former U.S. Attorney General Janet Reno and actor Michael J. Fox. It's believed that Parkinson's, along with long-term methamphetamine use, reduces the level of the chemical dopamine in the brain.

For some chronic methamphetamine users, dopamine function is never restored. A study conducted by NIDA director Nora D. Volkow at the Brookhaven National Laboratory in Upton, New York, examined brain scans and tests of motor skills and memory administered to 15 recovering addicts. All of the study participants had used crystal a minimum of five days a week during a two-year period but had been clean for two months prior to the study. During the natural human aging process, the brain's production of dopamine decreases at a rate of 6% to 7% per decade. Brain scans of the subjects in the Brookhaven study showed the equivalent of 40 years of declining dopamine production.

Another study conducted by the Center for Substance

Abuse Prevention (CSAP) noted that there are two types of crystal users: those who ingest the drug recreationally and those who used crystal because they believe it makes them more productive and competent on the job. "For both types of methamphetamine users the outcome is bleak," the CSAP study said, citing other research that shows as much as 50% of dopamine-producing cells in the brain can be damaged even after using only small amounts of methamphetamine. The study says that the brain damage caused by crystal resembles the damage caused by strokes or Alzheimer's disease.

Different Routes, Same Destination

MethAbuse.net says, "When the user injects or smokes the drug, an intense but brief high results. If the user has snorted or taken the drug orally (by capsule), a longer-lasting high is the result rather than a brief rush." The heady rush experienced by crystal IV-users and smokers is due to the fact that the drug mimics the effect of the body's natural production of adrenaline. Both adrenaline and crystal increase heart rate, blood pressure, and breathing.

Brent, a car salesman in Cleveland, used to inject crystal, but he preferred smoking it. He disagrees with the claim that both injecting and smoking provide an instant rush. "An injection is immediate and a much more intense high than smoking. Smoking mellows you out, comparatively speaking," Brent says. "I was smart enough to know the dangers of having someone else who is high injecting me."

Crystal users feel an immediate, intense euphoria after smoking or injecting the drug. Eating crystal, rubbing it on the gums, or swallowing it in pill form are less powerful means of ingestion. Taking crystal by these means delays by 15 to 20 minutes the blissful high that crystal smokers and IV-users enjoy almost instantly. Snorting crystal (also known as "insufflation") produces a less powerful burst of euphoria that usually lasts three to five minutes. Although snorting and oral ingestion don't produce the dramatic high of smoking or injecting, the high from taking meth nasally or orally lasts longer—up to 12 hours.

Yet another way of ingesting crystal is called "hot-railing." The user heats up a glass tube with a butane lighter, then inhales crystal through the red-hot glass tube. "As the crystal travels up the tube, it turns into smoke, which is then absorbed by the lining in your nose. I prefer hot-railing. It's my favorite," says Jonathan, a masseur and part-time bartender in Long Beach, California. Describing hot-railing so dramatically triggered Jonathan's desire to use that he terminated the interview soon after he brought up the subject.

Chris, a recovering crystal addict who posted a letter on CrystalRecovery.com's letters page, also prefers to hot-rail crystal. His infatuation with the drug began when a buddy offered him a bump of crystal, which led him to do "line after line after line." Within weeks of his first exposure, he became a self-described crystal addict.

Drug use ravished his life. Because of crystal, Chris lost his job, got kicked out of his apartment, and ended up living in his car in downtown Atlanta. Somehow, he found ways, which he doesn't elaborate on in his posting, to get crystal for free. He began a 10-month binge and stayed up all the time except for occasional "cat naps" that lasted only two hours.

Staying high for so long made him dangerously sleep-deprived. Once, while driving his car in the express lane of a freeway, he began fading in and out of consciousness.

After he passed out, he later learned, his car flipped over four times and the engine caught fire. A good Samaritan broke the car's sunroof window and pulled him out of the burning wreck.

While Chris was recuperating in a hospital, the police searched the remains of his car and found a small amount of crystal that had survived the fire. In Georgia possession of crystal, no matter how small the amount, is a felony. Suddenly, Chris found himself charged with both reckless driving and possession of methamphetamine; he got lucky, however, and ended up spending only a few days in the county jail and 17 in a psychiatric hospital.

Soon after the hospital cut him loose, Chris began to attend Narcotics Anonymous meetings. "I am feeling so good today," he reports in an interview. "Although doing meth numbed a lot of the bad shit going on with me, it numbed the good too. My brain is finally detoxing, and I'm enjoying life more than I ever thought I could without using [crystal] all the damn time." He proudly adds that he will soon have accrued 30 days of sobriety. As for crystal, he says, "Fuck meth! That shit about killed my ass!"

Poor Scores

In a study conducted by Brown University in which 52% of the participants used methamphetamine one to three times every day, meth users scored worse than a control group on the recall of words and pictures, psychomotor speed, the manipulation of information, the ability to focus on a task and ignore irrelevant information, and the ability to engage in abstract thinking.

IV users scored the worst. While there was no dramatic difference in scores among long-term users and participants who had begun using crystal more recently, frequency of use did affect cognitive performance. Daily users were more impaired than occasional users, and not surprisingly, the worst abusers—those who ingested the drug 10 times a day or more—experienced the worst cognitive impairment.

Losing Teeth Over It

The Sacramento Bee reports that crystal users may "age prematurely and their teeth may rot." The phenomenon of rotting teeth is called "drug-induced osteoporosis." Osteoporosis makes teeth and bones brittle and prone to breaking. A recovering crystal addict who calls himself "D" posted a note on CrystalRecovery.com's letters page that explained why crystal addicts have dental problems: "Meth absorbs calcium." Besides rotting his teeth, crystal caused "D" to suffer three heart attacks during the time when he was snorting or smoking a fourth of a gram daily. "I was an especially heavy user," he says.

"D" had been clean and sober for nine months when he posted his message on CrystalRecovery.com, but because his excessive drug use has left him physically devastated, his sobriety wasn't a happy ending. Due to meth-induced osteoporosis, "D" is constantly sore: Some days he finds it impossible to walk due to pain in his "greatly deteriorated" pelvis, hips, and spine. He says he feels like an 80-year-old even though he is only 24. He finds consolation in his doctor's assertion that osteoporosis is reversible, although after nine months of sobriety his health had still not improved.

To those who remain in crystal's thrall, "D" offers a health tip: "Please, if you're using, it's a good idea to take two 600-milligram tablets of calcium a day just to keep yourself healthy so that once you quit you do not get my agonizingly painful bone disorder."

That is advice "No Teeth" may have wished he took before he earned his nickname on QuitMeth.com. Although "No Teeth" has been off crystal for a year, he's still paying the price for his addiction. "We never took care of ourselves when we were doing meth, man. No food, no water, no sleep. No wonder I had to have five teeth pulled last week, because meth wrecked all the enamel in my teeth to the point where my teeth were hollowed out and full of holes," he writes. "No Teeth" laments that he will have to put up with his mouthful of rotten teeth until he can afford "$1,000 or so to buy new teeth. Meanwhile, I'll look like a tweaker" despite his yearlong sobriety.

Dental problems seem inevitable for longtime users. Los Angeles drug counselor Mark Hufford, who got sober eight years ago, recalls, "I lost 15 teeth as a result of neglecting my oral hygiene." Rotten teeth are "pretty common among meth users, who have lots of dental problems."

The Man in the Mirror

Vanity, among other issues, has motivated Jonathan, the bartender and masseur, to seek sobriety. With the physique of a competitive bodybuilder, Jonathan is a genuine head-turner, and one of the things he hates most about his crystal runs is that they make him lose hard-won muscle weight. Although he usually only loses a few pounds during a binge, Jonathan suffers from a bit of body dysmorphic order (a negative self-image typical of anorexics) and imagines that the minor weight loss has turned him into a skeleton. "Guys are shocked when I come down because of my weight loss, the gauntness in my face. People see me as a muscular guy, but when I'm on crystal, I shrink [by] five to 10 pounds."

Jonathan feels insulted when friends point out his weight loss. "They're shocked by the way I look. I think that's mean. I don't judge them for being fat or whatever. They go, 'Jonathan!' and I say, 'I'm human too.'"

As a bartender, Jonathan feels as though he is on display and that people can tell when he's on a crystal binge because of his weight loss. "I try not to do crystal while I'm bartending because I don't want people to see what I look like when I'm on crystal. I want them to see the real me, the person everyone likes, the person who cares for other people. On crystal, I'm narrow-minded, selfish, and I don't have much to give except sex."

Masculinity issues has also motivated Jonathan to stop using crystal. Although he prides himself on being a dominant top (the insertive partner in anal sex), crystal lowers his testosterone level, Jonathan believes, and turns him into a voracious bottom (the receptive partner). "I hate the fact that I'm a bottom," Jonathan says. "It lets people take advantage of you. You lose all sense of dignity. Sex becomes nasty. Crystal brings out the worst in people."

Crystal use hasn't been a completely negative experience for Jonathan, although he can point to only one time when he felt its beneficial effects. Five years ago, he shared crystal with a sex partner at a bathhouse. His sex partner, a stranger, then treated Jonathan to a 15-day luxury trip to Hong Kong. "On rare occasions, crystal has opened a door that normally would never open for me. The trip to Hong Kong was the trip of a lifetime."

Jonathan normally practices safer sex, but when he's taking crystal all his resolve goes up in smoke. "I let people come up my ass without a rubber," he admits. "I hate that about crystal." Although he seroconverted at the amazingly young age of 17, Jonathan remains in excellent health, except for a tendency to contract upper respiratory infections, which is another common problem among crystal users, especially for those who smoke the drug. "I've had HIV for 18 years now," Jonathan says. "It would be sad if, after surviving AIDS, I ended up dying from crystal!"

Saved by the Hell

John's flirtation with methamphetamine was brief but almost fatal. After a nine-month binge in 2002, the 32-year-old lost his clerical job, his boyfriend, and his health—and came perilously close to joining the ranks of the homeless.

"I have a degree in journalism, and I've always been curious about things," John says. He wanted to know what the big deal about crystal was, so he tried it. He soon found himself sucked into an alluring subculture of drugs and sex.

John hit bottom in a dramatic way. While crashing at the end of a sleepless six-day binge, he got into an argument with his boyfriend. The confrontation escalated until his boyfriend threatened to kill him.

As the drug left his system, John became severely depressed and e-mailed a suicide note to 20 friends. Only one of the e-mail recipients thought to call the cops, who took John to a hospital's psychiatric unit for observation.

Released after only 24 hours, John made the mistake of telling his supervisor at work the reason for his hospitalization. He also confided that his boyfriend had threatened to kill him. His supervisor told her boss, who fired John, citing "Way too much drama."

Crystal was especially attractive to John because he

has had a weight problem for most of his life. In 2000, his 6-foot-2 frame carried around 300 pounds. Two years later, thanks to exercise and regular weekend crystal binges where he'd typically snort an "eight-ball" (four grams of methamphetamine), John had shed 100 pounds. He didn't mind that he had developed what he calls "fish face"—gaunt, sunken cheeks that led coworkers to suspect he had a terminal illness—because after a lifetime of dieting, John finally felt lean and muscular.

But his colleagues were onto something. John always had unprotected sex while high on crystal, and during a nine-month binge, he seroconverted and began to show the facial wasting common to HIV-positive patients. John says, "Crystal turned me into a raging sexaholic. Friends called me the 'Energizer Bottom' because I just kept going and going. I could only have sex if I was high, and I never used a condom."

Life at home was as chaotic as it was at work. John's emotionally and physically abusive boyfriend was also addicted to crystal and unemployed. John made only $11 an hour at time. "I went broke trying to support both of us and our habit," he says.

John's roommate (not his boyfriend) finally did a one-man intervention in response to the deterioration of John's health and physical appearance. "I'm tired of coming home every night and seeing you in this condition. It breaks my heart. You're going to the clinic tomorrow," his roommate told him. A positive HIV test at the clinic confirmed what John had already suspected; he'd been waking up in night sweats, a common symptom of HIV and AIDS.

A relentless optimist despite the wreckage in his life, John believes everything happens for a reason and credits his drug addiction with saving his life: "I never would have gotten tested [for HIV] if I hadn't gone to rehab."

Although John has Kaposi's sarcoma, he has responded well to HAART (highly active antiretroviral therapy), or "the cocktail," which often includes protease inhibitors. John proudly posts his HIV lab results on his AOL home page, which says that his viral load, a measure of the virus in his blood, is 739, and his CD4 T cell count (white blood cells that fight disease, also called helper cells) is 522. (AIDS-related illnesses usually don't begin to occur until the count of CD4 T cells falls below 250.)

The final chapter on John's dangerous dalliance with methamphetamine has yet to be written. John never sought the help of a 12-step program such as Crystal Meth Anonymous, and although he describes himself as "clean and sober," he admits that he has snorted crystal four times since he was last hospitalized. It remains to be seen if John's current abstinence is permanent or only represents a stay of execution.

Crash and Burn

Users report that the dysphoria they experience as they come down from crystal is extraordinarily uncomfortable—and clearly inconvenient. Paul, 36, a masseur in Laguna Beach, California, says he finally stopped using crystal "because I don't have the time to deal with the crash."

Some try to evade the crash by taking even larger doses of the drug as their brain develops a tolerance to it and needs more to stay high. Others switch from the less potent methods of imbibing like snorting or eating to the more powerful forms of smoking or injecting the drug.

Binges can involve consuming the drug every two to three hours over a period of days or weeks—often with little or no sleep required or even possible. The binge typically ends when the user runs out of the drug or is too disoriented by the incipient crash to make another drug score. At worst, binges can lead to psychotic behavior, uncontrollable anger, and outbursts of physical violence.

Dan, a Cedar Rapids, Iowa, resident in his 50s, estimates that he blew a quarter of a million dollars on crystal in less than a year. He has also witnessed the violence crystal wreaks firsthand—he was almost raped by a man who followed him home from a bar. Dan's guest began their "date" by hitting him repeatedly, "but not that hard," Dan recalls, adding, "He had a hundred pounds on me, and as soon as he started hitting me I stopped resisting,"

The man then tried to penetrate Dan, but fortunately his attacker suffered from "crystal dick" (impotence). Thinking fast, Dan offered to perform oral sex on his tormentor. But instead of a blow job, Dan "bit [his assailant's] dick so hard it bled." While the man screamed in agony and immobility, Dan made his escape.

Tweaking Lab Rats

Animal studies have shown that even low doses of methamphetamine over an extended period of time can reduce the brain's natural production of dopamine by 50%. Conversely, a single high dose given to laboratory animals damaged nerve endings in the dopamine-producing region of the brain called the ventral tegmental area. Long-term use also damaged 50% of the nerve cells that produce dopamine.

Other studies cited by *The Official Patient's Sourcebook on Methamphetamine Dependence* reveal that the natural production of serotonin, another neurotransmitter that regulates pleasure in the brain, is also decreased by chronic use of crystal. The decrease in the brain's natural pleasure-causing neurotransmitters prolongs the crash. "With the depletion of neurotransmitters you can get long-term depression," says drug counselor Joni Lavick.

NIDA cites another round of animal studies that found that even after two months of abstinence lab animals given crystal still suffered reduced levels of dopamine, which caused slower motor skills and weakened memory. But the recovery picture isn't entirely bleak, even for long-term users: After nine months of abstinence, test subjects showed an increase in dopamine production, but they still suffered impairments in motor skills and memory.

The Crumbling Architecture of the Brain

The release of yet another neurotransmitter—endorphins, which cause the "jogger's high" or euphoria that follows an intense workout— is blocked after prolonged use of crystal. UCLA's Bayrd says, "After you have used for a while, the only pleasure you can derive in life comes from further drug use. A lovely day, a balmy breeze— [crystal users] no longer derive pleasure from ordinary sources. Crystal becomes the only physiological source of pleasure.

"That's one of the reasons it's so hard to get off the drug. Users feel so miserable. Nothing gives them pleasure. It makes them anhedonic [unable to experience pleasure]. That's the cruelest [aspect of crystal use]. We need to derive a little pleasure out of everyday life. It's the sustaining thing in our daily life. The inability to derive pleasure from anything else is the truly insidious thing about meth use. It starts out as an additive to pleasure, and soon it's the only source of ecstatic feelings—and they're plenty ecstatic."

UCLA psychiatry professor Thomas Newton also notes the joylessness of the chronic drug user. "Crystal causes a malfunction in the brain's reward system. People who use meth say that without it they have very little positive feeling. They keep taking meth to get the normal feeling [of joy] back." Newton adds that it can take several years for the brain to return to normal functioning—especially if drug use was long-term.

Crystal intake also makes you less intelligent. In one NIDA study, 40 crystal users, 40 cocaine users, and 80 members of a drug-free control group participated in tests that gauged memory and learning abilities. Not surprisingly, meth users scored more poorly than the control group on tests of word recall, perceptual speed, the ability to manipulate information, and abstract thinking. Cocaine users came in second. "Overall, both drugs are associated with similar cognitive deficits," the NIDA study reported. "The most striking difference is that methamphetamine abusers have more trouble than cocaine abusers with tasks requiring attention and the ability to organize information."

Urban Legends

Crystal causes other skin problems, such as "speed bumps," which are abscesses that occur under the skin when intravenous users miss a vein and inject the drug subcutaneously. One urban legend is that some desperate crystal addicts will prick their speed bumps to get to the liquid crystal underneath the inflamed skin and smoke it. CrystalRecovery.com's Webmaster writes, "I have not seen any proof that the liquid in speed bumps is meth. It may be just puss" that desperate addicts harvest and smoke.

At QuitMeth.com, someone whose e-mail handle is "No Teeth" writes that he originally believed his skin lesions were caused by crab lice, or "chiggers" as he called them. No Teeth was later told that the crystal his body could not absorb was excreted through his pores: "We were so dehydrated that our bodies were trying to get rid of the poison any way it could by sweating it out." No Teeth said the sweat came out "real greasy and thick," which blocked his pores and caused more blistering. CrystalRecovery.com also labels as an urban legend the claim that crystal users smell because the drug seeps out of their pores. A more likely explanation is that the addict is simply too disoriented to bathe during a binge.

Up to 25% of crystal cannot be absorbed and is excreted in urine. Another urban legend is that truly needy meth users save and dry their own urine in order to resmoke the residue in the urine. As Thomas Newton has pointed out, "Once somebody gets into crystal, they're just going to go down the toilet."

—4—
The Toll on the Soul: Meth and Madness

"I NOW HAVE EXTREME PARANOIA. I FIND IT
HARD TO TRUST ANYBODY AND AM ALWAYS
ON MY GUARD."

—MATT, 18

"I WENT STARK RAVING MAD.... AT FIRST YOU
REALIZE THE DRUG IS MAKING YOU THINK
THINGS, THEN YOU STOP REMEMBERING
THAT IT'S THE CRYSTAL, NOT REALITY. I'VE
KNOWN SO MANY PEOPLE TREATED FOR PSY-
CHOSIS WHEN THEIR REAL PROBLEM WAS
METH ADDICTION."

—MEL, 38

"CRYSTAL ALMOST INDUCES PARANOID
SCHIZOPHRENIC BEHAVIOR."

—MICHAEL MAJESKI, CLINICAL PSYCHOLOGIST

"I AM SORRY. I CAN'T STOP USING THIS EVIL
DRUG."

—RAY, 25 (FROM HIS SUICIDE NOTE)

It's difficult to say which is more debilitating: the physical or psychological devastation crystal causes. Chronic users can experience psychotic episodes as well as paranoia, anxiety, disorientation, and insomnia. Crystal addicts also suffer from progressive social and occupational deterioration. *The Official Patient's Sourcebook on Methamphetamine Dependence* reports that psychotic behavior "can sometimes persist for months or years after [drug] use has ceased."

The National Institute on Drug Abuse reports that "methamphetamine users can have episodes of violent behavior, paranoia, anxiety, confusion, and insomnia," and a variety of experts say violence often accompanies crystal use. In 2000, the FBI investigated two dramatic cases of meth madness. One involved a crystal addict who commandeered an armored tank from a National

Guard armory and proceeded to crush every car in sight with his vehicle. In New Mexico, a seriously tweaking man beheaded his son while hallucinating that the boy was Satan.

Missouri prosecutor Cynthia Rushefsky offers an explanation for all this meth-induced mayhem: "The violence is increasing, I think, because the purity of the dope is increasing."

"Zombies and Soulless Addicts"

Matt is 18 and a self-described "meth addict" who finds himself enmeshed in the binge-and-crash cycle of crystal addiction. In a sad posting on the KCI message board, he writes that after amassing one month of white-knuckle sobriety he "was back into the cycle— smoking, tweaking, crashing, smoking, tweaking, etc. All day, every day, all we did was smoke." He confesses that he was "spun out of my mind" when he posted his message.

Matt's introduction to drug use began in the 10th grade and consisted of smoking marijuana and dropping acid. At 16, he befriended a local man who ran a small methamphetamine lab, and thus Matt's destructive entanglement with the drug began. He got into the habit of smoking the drug at the man's lab late into the night and the following morning. After just a week of this regimen, Matt lost 20 pounds.

Then the man who ran the lab got busted, and Matt used the opportunity to stop using crystal for a month— until he found another drug dealer. Matt seems a bit opaque when he tries to explain just how a teenager could afford such an expensive daily habit: "We would 'gather' money and just go smoke [crystal] all day and tweak out on whatever we could find."

Matt did not remain in denial about having a drug problem for long. "I never looked at myself as an addict, but I soon realized it when I would just sit around waiting for my dealer to bring me some 'go.'" Then, after a three-day nonstop crystal binge, Matt and his drug buddies attempted what he describes as "one of the most stupid things we had ever done." Matt doesn't offer any specific details other than that his friend ended up being arrested for possession of cocaine, and Matt and two other friends were jailed for participation in "organized crime." (Matt never dealt drugs, but he may have had so much crystal in his possession when he was busted that he qualified as a dealer and was charged under drug-racketeering statutes used to nab major traffickers.)

When Matt got out of jail, he managed to go another month without crystal, but then he found another dealer conveniently located "right down the street." He spent more than $500 on a monthlong binge.

At the time of the posting, Matt said he was "just a skeleton of 120 pounds at 5 foot 11." Proving that self-knowledge isn't enough ammunition to stop using drugs, Matt diagnoses himself as suffering "the beginnings of methamphetamine psychosis. I now have extreme paranoia. I find it hard to trust anybody and am always on my guard."

Crystal has turned Matt and his drug companions into what he calls "zombies and soulless addicts." The past year, he says, has been a "blur" of binging, but he acknowledges his problem with commendable clarity. "I know the dope has taken a toll on my soul and brain. I still use all the time. I want to quit, but I just can't find the strength."

A Lifetime of Withdrawal

Drug cravings, loss of energy, depression, fearfulness, somnolence or insomnia, shaking, nausea, sweating, hyperventilation, and increased appetite: According to the Web site for the Dana Point, California–based treatment center, Solutions for Recovery (www.solutions4recovery.com), "these symptoms can commonly last several weeks" after drug use ceases; however, "the severity and length of the symptoms vary with the amount of damage done" to the user's physical chemistry.

According to *The Official Patient's Sourcebook on Methamphetamine Disorders,* the length of the period of withdrawal is determined by how long and how much of the drug the user has done. Longtime users may never get over the effects of withdrawal, condemning them to a life of panic, paranoia, and all the other debilitating symptoms of withdrawal. Psychologist Michael Majeski says the binge-and-crash cycle typical of longtime hard-core crystal users resembles an artificially or chemically induced case of manic depression (bipolar disorder), complete with manic highs and depressive lows.

Specialist Neva Chauppette makes the point, in fact, that people with bipolar disorder are drawn to crystal: "Some of my clients have psychiatric illnesses that predispose them to [using crystal]: bipolar disorder, sex addiction, and ADHD. There's more in the 'mix' than just wanting to get high and hot. If you're bipolar to begin with, crystal will 'treat' the depression associated with a bipolar 'low.' If they're already manic before they start using crystal, they may want to extend the manic episode with crystal. It's quite the high," Chauppette says.

According to a 2000 report from the FBI, chronic meth

abusers typically ingest large amounts of crystal every two or three hours during binges in which the user doesn't sleep for more than a week. Sleep deprivation, the FBI points out, causes the user to suffer extreme irritability, severe agitation, anxiety, paranoia, hallucinations, and violent or unpredictable behavior. In some ways the side effects of crystal resemble those of cocaine, but the crystal high lasts longer, between six and 14 hours per dose.

Tsunamis of Pleasure

Both the initial rush and the prolonged high from crystal occur because the drug artificially stimulates and floods the reward centers of the brain with the pleasure-inducing neurotransmitter dopamine. This gusher of dopamine short-circuits the body's natural survival instincts. The brain's hunger, sleep, and thirst centers shut down because of the increased amount of dopamine in the brain during the period of crystal use.

It's interesting to note that many prescription antidepressants like Prozac also elevate dopamine levels in the brain—but without the dramatic highs or crippling lows caused by crystal.

While the short-term effects of crystal use range from unpleasant to annoying, the long-term effects underline the severe dangers of using this drug. Over the long haul, crystal can cause mood disturbances, dramatic mood swings, and repetitive motor activity, among other side effects already listed.

Playing With Guns

Mel, the West Hollywood waiter-actor, began to hallucinate after an eight-day binge with almost no sleep. "That's the longest binge I ever had, and that was the week I went stark raving mad," he recalls. During his psychotic episode, Mel heard voices telling him to leave Los Angeles and not contact anyone he knew. "I felt compelled to get out of town."

Somehow, despite his debilitated state after not sleeping for more than a week, Mel managed to make his way to Union Station in Los Angeles. While waiting for a train out of town, he saw some street musicians performing for tips—but he thought their instruments were guns. "I thought they were weapons, not guitars. I believed that if I didn't get on a train, they'd shoot me," he says.

One of the insidious elements of crystal use is that after a while, the drug user forgets it's the crystal that's causing hallucination. "At first you realize the drug is making you think things," Mel says. Then you stop remembering that it's the crystal, not reality. I've known so many people treated for psychosis when their real problem was meth addiction."

Mel was one of the lucky ones: Somehow, he managed to realize that the voices he heard were delusional, and instead of boarding a train at Union Station, he went home. He attributes this clarity to his participation in a 12-step program before he resumed using crystal.

The incident in the train station 10 years ago represented Mel's bottom. "I started going to [12-step] meetings, and I've been sober ever since. But I had to be scared out of my mind by those musicians wielding 'weapons.'" Mel warns crystal users that if they don't seek help, eventually they will begin to hallucinate. "It happens to all crystal users if they use enough," he says.

Mel is grateful to the recovering crystal users who got together and created Crystal Meth Anonymous, during his first year of sobriety. "I really got involved with CMA. It saved my life."

Foiling a Russian Plot

Clinical psychologist Michael Majeski encountered chemically induced paranoia firsthand, over 14 years ago, in the days before he got clean and sober. While flying on crystal, he set up a date with a man who had no history of mental illness, but by the time the two got together, the man was hallucinating that Russians were spying on him. "He had foil on all of his walls in order to interrupt the [Russians'] signals so they couldn't find him. You see the same exact behavior with paranoid schizophrenics. Crystal almost induces paranoid schizophrenic behavior," Majeski says.

Evaporating Inhibition

Los Angeles psychologist Guy Baldwin attributes crystal's popularity in large part to what he calls its "disinhibiting" effect—a term almost every drug expert and counselor interviewed for this book used. Crystal, Baldwin explains, relieves the user of sexual problems or hang-ups he may have while sober. "My guess is that the current popularity of crystal has a lot to do with the fact that the drug is erotically disinhibiting. It allows people to behave in ways that they have always longed to behave but have not been able to without the influence of drugs," says Baldwin, who estimates that a quarter of his patients are crystal addicts. "Because of the disinhibitional qualities of [crystal], people will often attempt to live out fantasies that put them in life-threatening situations, apart from unsafe sex."

"Treatment for Stimulant Use Disorders: Methamphetamine and Cocaine," a 1999 article published by the Substance Abuse and Mental Health Services Administration's Center for Substance Abuse Treatment

(SAMHSA-CSAT) in Washington, D.C., confirms Baldwin's claim about the connection between crystal use and disinhibited sex: "Research has revealed an association between stimulant use and a variety of compulsive sexual behaviors." The article lists examples such as "promiscuous and unprotected sex, compulsive masturbation, and compulsive pornographic viewing" and also claims that crystal and cocaine use can promote homosexual behavior by heterosexuals.

"I was seven years sober when diagnosed with AIDS [in February 2000]. It wasn't a surprise because of my behavior when using," Mel says. "That's just part of the disinhibiting nature of crystal. If somebody wants to fuck you without a condom, you just don't care."

Mel says he is "completely healthy" these days: "My viral load is undetectable, and my [CD4] T cell count is 650." Mel wouldn't be enjoying his current health, he believes, if he hadn't stopped using crystal. "People need to know: Crystal eats T cells for breakfast, lunch, and dinner."

Brent, the Cleveland automobile salesperson, also noticed the disinhibiting effect crystal had on his behavior: "I'd do things on crystal I would have thought twice about if I had been sober—like multiple partners, unprotected sex, getting double-fucked." By "getting double-fucked," Brent means having two penises inserted in his rectum at the same time.

"Meth is intense. It allows disinhibition to run rampant," says Neva Chauppette. One of Guy Baldwin's patients had always fantasized about running naked outside. On crystal, the fantasy came true, and the patient was arrested and prosecuted. "So a person with no prior criminal record ended up having one. He served time in prison," Baldwin says.

Synthetic Paranoia

Tweakers sometimes exhibit the characteristics of the paranoid schizophrenic. "I've seen a lot of paranoia [among patients] that can last for a couple of days to a couple of years. These are patients who had no history of schizophrenia or paranoia before they began using crystal," Michael Majeski says.

Before he got sober six years ago, Tim, a former porn star and prostitute who lives in the Silver Lake district of Los Angeles, had also lost touch with reality and endured terrifying auditory hallucinations. "My whole mental state was gone or not working properly," he says. Tim imagined that he could hear people outside his apartment, including the FBI. He also heard invisible people calling him by name, surreptitiously photographing him, and watching him through gaps in the fence that surrounded his apartment building.

Mark Hufford, a recovering addict who is now a senior drug counselor at the Hollywood Recovery Center, only hallucinated once when was he was using crystal. His many binges lasted up to five days, but "the paranoia was constant. The delusion that people were plotting against me was constant," Mark says.

Will, the Webmaster for Crystal Meth Anonymous, had no history of paranoia until he hit bottom on crystal. "My bottom had to do with paranoid psychosis caused by a meth overdose," Will says. He suffered from delusions that his phones were tapped and there were hidden cameras in his home—as well as auditory hallucinations. "I believed things were happening that weren't," Will says.

Realizing, despite his impaired mental state, that he had a major problem with crystal use, Will tried white-knuckle sobriety and managed to remain sober on his own for nine months before relapsing. When his lover finally demanded that Will seek professional help, he checked into a psychiatric and drug rehab clinic on an inpatient basis, where he spent 28 days, followed by six months in a sober-living house.

But even after seven months of sobriety, the toxic after-effects of crystal use persisted. "Crystal impacted my ability to focus and concentrate. I had short-term memory loss for an entire year after I quit," Will says. The auditory and visual hallucinations he had experienced while on crystal continued for months after he quit. "They lessened with time. It was like slowly turning the volume down on your stereo," Will says.

Crystal impacted Will's career as a Web designer. While he was using, especially when he hit bottom, he had to refer lucrative Web-designing jobs to colleagues after crystal made him too disoriented to finish assignments he had started. The drug also made him give up his real passion, writing fiction. Will had moved to Los Angeles to enroll in the film program at the University of Southern California; he had hoped to write the "great American screenplay." Since getting clean, he has started writing again, although these days he writes novels and a column for a magazine based on the East Coast.

Despite the psychotic episodes he suffered, Will considers himself lucky. Although he engaged in a great deal of unprotected sex while high, often to please a partner, Will remains HIV-negative, a rarity among Crystal Meth Anonymous members. "Most guys in CMA are HIV-positive because crystal lowers your inhibitions about safe sex and sharing needles," he says

Will attributes his good luck to the fact that most of

his unsafe sex occurred with a deeply closeted, married member of the military, which requires regular HIV testing. If you test positive for HIV, you're automatically honorably discharged from the service. To decrease his chances of seroconverting, Will's army buddy only had sex with Will. "In retrospect, we were both delusional," says Will, "but I never did seroconvert."

One of the benefits of getting off crystal was a major improvement in Will's health. While using, he experienced chronic sinus infections. "I was just sick with sinus infections the whole time I was using." This may have been because he snorted the drug or because his dealer adding toxins to increase his supply of crystal—or simply because the drug lowered his resistance. Since Will has been off the drug, he has gone years without even getting a cold—and no more paranoia.

The Face of Addiction

Nick pulls up in a preposterously large Mercedes that's so new it doesn't have license plates. In his mid 30s, Nick is a successful attorney who works as a controller for a Fortune 500 company.

It's Monday morning, but Nick isn't at work. He's crashing after a weekend binge of snorting methamphetamine, so he called in sick to work. Instead of crunching numbers, he's cruising a popular pickup place behind one of West Hollywood's less glamorous gay bars.

Even though Nick's body aches because the drugs are leaving his system, this isn't why he's playing hooky; it's because of the holes in his face, or more accurately, the holes he thinks are in his face. In fact, his complexion is flawless, a perfect cocoa-butter shade without a blemish.

Male-model handsome, he looks like a young Paul Newman, and his tan is so deep a passerby asks Nick if he just got back from Hawaii.

"No," he explains, "I'm wearing that makeup people with scars put on their face. Remember that model, Marla Hansen?" (Hansen is the New Yorker whose landlord slashed her face with a razor in 1986 after she turned him down for a date.) "She used to be a TV spokesmodel for that makeup. It worked for her."

And it's apparently working for Nick, who looks drop-dead gorgeous if you ignore his exceedingly tired eyes. Nick may not have any scars yet, but he's terrified he will get some. Whenever he begins to crash on methamphetamine, an obsessive-compulsive disorder called formication overwhelms him, and he feels compelled to pick at imaginary zits on his face. According to CrystalRecovery.com, this is a common phenomenon among crystal users who "may scratch themselves or pick at sores until they become infected."

A patron standing outside the bar eavesdrops on our conversation and tries to pick up Nick by telling him his coloring looks like a genuine tan, but Nick is inconsolable. In addition to his own private hell of mutilating his face, he's suffering from one of the more common symptoms of methamphetamine withdrawal: what psychologists call "dysphoria" and users call "crashing." The crash ranges from mild to severe, and at the moment Nick's definitely dangling on the deep end of the continuum of emotional pain.

Although he's not suicidal, Nick is extremely depressed— after all, he thinks he has just pockmarked his face. Self-mutilation is only one of the reasons for his despair, however. After a night of partying at various bars the night before, Nick picked up a nice young man at an after-hours place, and they went back to the man's apartment.

Maybe if Nick hadn't been so disoriented by drugs, he would have noticed the man's odd behavior, which became downright psychotic after they had sex. At that point, the man identified himself as a prostitute and demanded payment. He also started mumbling something unintelligible about taking Nick back to jail with him; he claimed he had just gotten out of prison.

Paranoid from drugs and the dangerous situation he found himself in, Nick panicked. Instead of telling the prostitute to get out, Nick emptied his wallet on the man's couch and fled.

Imaginary Infestations

One of the more disturbing side effects of long-term abuse is the phenomenon of formication, which resembles the delirium tremens of longtime alcoholics and creates the delusion that one's skin is infested with insects or parasites. Chronic users imagine bugs are crawling all over them. Nick was engaging in a variation of formication when he hallucinated that his face was pockmarked with holes.

West Hollywood actor Mel says there's a certain reality to the delusions caused by formication. While high, users "get these obsessive thoughts. Tweakers stare in the mirror and pick at what they think are scabs. Eventually, the scabs become real because you've picked at your face."

Formication is so terrifying that it can scare addicts straight. The online crystal rehab resource QuitMeth.com has a sublink titled "Meth Monsters," which is devoted to nightmarish crystal experiences. One recovering addict who signed his posting "Nobody" said he was so certain the imaginary insects were real and not a hallucination that he went to a hospital emergency room for treatment. "Nobody" doesn't record the reaction of the E.R. doctors to his delusion, but he does say the incident brought him to the point where "I finally decided that I had had enough of this drug. What an insane bad trip that was, don't you think?"

In response to "Nobody's" request for others to share whether they'd had similar hallucinations, someone who calls himself "CRG" attested to how real formication can seem: "I have blown inchworms out of my nose. In reality it was snot, but you couldn't convince me of that when it was happening."

Lethal Thoughts

In the "Stimulants" chapter of *The Treatment of Substance Abuse,* the authors write, "The depression of the crash can be extremely intense and may include potentially lethal, but temporary, suicidal ideation [obsessive thoughts about committing suicide], which remit completely when the crash is over. This transient state can occur in individuals who have no prior history of depression or of suicidal ideation or suicide attempts." The book also reports that for a small number of crystal users, the depression remains even after the user has completely withdrawn from the drug.

Ted, 38, a telemarketer in Dallas, believes his crystal use was a "coping mechanism" that helped him deal with chronic depression, which he has suffered from since he was 16. It was at that age that Ted made his first of 11 suicide attempts. "I never tried to commit suicide when I was high," he says.

Ted seroconverted during marathon sex sessions that typically lasted three days with no sleep. Contracting HIV in March 2002 may have been another suicide attempt, he suspects. "I wasn't trying to have unsafe sex, but part of me wanted to contract HIV because at least then I'd have an end date to the struggles I've had with depression. I was too chicken to commit suicide, and subconsciously, I think I was trying to commit suicide with crystal," says the needle-phobic IV-user, who relied on friends to inject him with crystal.

Although the drug alleviated his suicidal ideation, it couldn't stop Ted from hitting bottom, which occurred while he was talking to his father during one of their weekly phone conversations. His father was a recovering alcoholic who had been hospitalized three times for the disease. Ted is certain his father knew he was high during their talks. "I usually called my father when I was crashing," Ted says. "On three different occasions in the middle of our conversation, my father excused himself and said he had to walk the dog. It broke his heart to hear me while I was high."

Crystal made Ted agoraphobic, and it got worse after he quit using in July 2003. "I was afraid to be seen in public. I couldn't even walk my dog." Ted spent the first week of sobriety curled up in a fetal position. He jumped whenever the phone rang, and "I dreaded any kind of human interaction."

It took Ted another two weeks before he was able to walk his long-suffering dog. "Before I started doing crystal, I used to take a three-mile hike with my dog every day," Ted says. Five months into his sobriety, he finally summoned up the energy to resume his workouts. "Once I was back at gym, I felt like I had reassembled myself," he repeats. Despite seroconverting, Ted says he's in perfect health and doesn't need to take AIDS medications.

Art Burn

Jeff's bottom occurred in the summer of 2003, when he was arrested in Hawaii after his dealer in Chicago sent him crystal via Federal Express. While in jail, he learned that all the artwork he had in storage and planned to use for the first exhibition of his silk-screen pieces had been sold at auction because no one had paid the storage fee.

Jeff waited until 3 A.M., when everyone else was asleep, and tied one end of a wet sheet around his neck and the other end to the bedpost, then rotated his body multiple times until the sheet choked him into unconsciousness.

By chance, a fellow inmate with whom Jeff had become friends woke up and went to the bathroom. He saw Jeff lying unconscious in his bed, untied the sheet, and performed CPR on Jeff. "He never told the authorities about my suicide attempt, which is good because I would have had to do prison time for that too," Jeff says.

Jeff now has almost four months of sobriety after spending three months in rehab. These days, he has an extra incentive to stay clean and participate in a 12-step program: After his arrest, he was sentenced to five years probation, which includes regular urine testing. If he fails a test, he will be sent back to prison for five years.

Rip Van Winkle in Rehab

On Yahoo's MethRecovery site, Pleasure Davis wrote that he's "tried all the programs: AA, NA, Fuckin' A, and a suicide attempt, in order to stop using crystal." Until he got sober in April 2003, Davis used the drug daily for two years, except for the three days he spent in a psychiatric ward after he tried to commit suicide by swallowing 50 tablets of the antidepressant Elavil.

Davis says he was emotionally and physically tired of making crystal the centerpiece of his life. He finally checked himself into a detox facility in April 2003, because he knew that the severe lethargy that accompanied withdrawal in the past would have prompted him to use again. But he was kicked out of the program after only four days in detox because he was too tired to perform the chores that make up part of the facility's treatment.

Paralyzing lethargy followed him from the detox ward to his parents' home, where he engaged in a Rip Van Winkle–like slumber. So far, despite bone-deep exhaustion, Davis has managed to achieve continuous sobriety for eight months. He offers encouragement and a warning to those who still use: "Don't give up. Don't let go. You will not stop until you're ready…or until you die."

Death by Meth

Ray's suicidal ideation was anything but transient. In fact, according to a KCI posting by his mother, crystal killed her son. Ray's mother, Linda, says that he was funny, smart, cute, honest, and a "happy guy to be around…until he started using meth." Ray battled his addiction demons for five years but finally lost the war when he was 25 years old.

Ray first tried to kill himself in July 2001 by injecting a massive dose of crystal, but that didn't work because his body had developed such a tolerance to the drug. By this time, crystal had ceased to be a pleasure-enhancing drug and Ray still felt suicidal, so he wrapped his dog's leash around a tree branch in his backyard and hung himself. Ray left a note that said, "I am sorry. I can't stop using this evil drug."

His mother remains inconsolable. In her posting she writes, "Meth killed my baby. I blame meth. Ray tried and tried and tried to get off of this drug. My life and many others are ruined because of meth. And my precious son died because of it!"

Going Down

Ron, 38, a photographer who resides in the Venice district of Los Angeles, suffered what he describes as "excruciating" depression while crashing on crystal. Depression made him so sensitive that "someone could look at me the wrong way, and I'd start crying." During withdrawal, Ron felt hopeless and suicidal.

Withdrawal also created physical problems. Ron was incoherent and slept "for days." His weight dropped from 200 pounds to an emaciated 140. Crystal users are often so intoxicated by the drug that they forget to drink water; Ron suffered severe dehydration. "I didn't drink water for days. When you're on crystal, you just don't think about things like drinking water." Dehydration caused more problems. "Skin tears very easily when you're dehydrated," Ron says. The skin between his toes became so dry he could hear the skin crackling when he walked. Ron also developed acne and began picking at his face.

Ron says his physical withdrawal is over, but he still has to deal with the guilt he feels about his behavior while high. "I have a lot of leftover emotional baggage about acting out sexually. I had no self-esteem. I went to sex clubs, bathhouses, had S/M sex with people I normally wouldn't have. I engaged in extreme-oriented sex, lots of anonymous and unprotected sex. Now I have to deal with my sexual acting out, all the people I hurt and lied to."

-5-
The Production of Poison

"Unlike more traditional drugs of abuse like heroin, cocaine, and marijuana, methamphetamine presents some unique challenges. First, it's synthetic, relying on no harvested crops for its manufacture, and unfortunately its recipe is relatively easy; anyone who can read and measure can make methamphetamine."
—Rogelio Guevara, Chief of Operations for the U.S. Drug Enforcement Administration

"Methamphetamine dealers exchange recipes like you and I would a cookie recipe."
—Sgt. Mark Nicastle of the North Metro Drug Task Force in Adams County, Colorado

"Addicts are working just as hard as Dow Chemical."
—Colorado drug treatment expert Eugene Strauber

Methamphetamine was developed in the early 1900s by changing the molecular structure of its precursor or parent drug, amphetamine. During World War II, German soldiers were given meth to keep them awake, elevate their mood, and suppress appetite. Instead of the dangerous and hard-to-get P2P version of meth, "Nazi dope," as it came to be called, used easily obtainable ephedrine as its base. Making meth from ephedrine was also much simpler than the P2P method.

In 1992, crystal made a comeback when Bob Paillet, the Thomas Edison of amateur meth manufacturing, left California and moved to Missouri. Researching the history of meth at a college library, Paillet, who had no formal training in chemistry, discovered the Nazis' recipe and probably shared it with other meth cooks during his glory days as the father of modern meth. His heyday didn't last long, however: He was arrested in 1993 and sentenced to five years probation.

A powerful central nervous stimulant, methamphetamine is a white, odorless, bitter-tasting crystalline substance that can be dissolved in both water and alcohol. An FBI bulletin in 2000 said that methamphetamine is "more potent" than its parent drug, amphetamine.

Hitler on Speed

Amphetamine was developed as a nasal decongestant and a bronchial dilator and is legally prescribed under the brand names Dexedrine, Benzedrine, and Methedrine. Amphetamines were first synthesized in Germany in 1887, although they didn't attract the attention of the medical establishment until the late 1920s, when the bronchial-dilating properties of the drug were discovered.

Soon doctors were prescribing amphetamines—without research to back up their enthusiasm—as panaceas for asthma, hay fever, depression, Parkinson's disease, epilepsy, travel sickness, night blindness, ADHD in children, obesity, narcolepsy, impotence, and the common cold. Amphetamines became so popular that eventually they could be bought as "pep pills" over the counter without a doctor's prescription.

Amphetamines and methamphetamines were both used in World War II, although only amphetamines were reportedly used by both the Axis and the Allies. It has been theorized that these pills fueled the quick and ferocious German invasions of Poland and France. Amphetamine.com speculates that the drug "sometimes caused states of quasipsychotic aggression in the combatants"—the perfect mindset for overrunning Europe and achieving world domination.

Hitler's own increasingly erratic behavior, as it became clear that Germany was losing the war, can be attributed to the treatments administered by Theodor Morell. Beginning in 1942, Dr. Morell injected the Nazi leader with nearly fatal daily doses of amphetamines.

But Hitler wasn't the only tweaker. John F. Kennedy also received amphetamine injections from a physician, and it has been theorized that the dangerous game of chicken which the 1962 Cuban Missile Crisis became was fueled by Kennedy's reckless drug-induced courage.

Despite the capacity of amphetamine to stimulate psychotic behavior, Dexedrine—nicknamed "go-pills"—is still prescribed to America pilots so they may stay awake during long-distance flights or arduous maneuvers. Some experts have speculated that one "friendly fire" incident in which several American soldiers were killed by other Americans in Iraq happened because the pilots tweaking on go-pills.

Cooking With Uncle Fester

It speaks volumes about the popularity of crystal meth that one of Amazon's top-selling books about the drug is a "cookbook" entitled *The Secrets of Methamphetamine Manufacture: Including Recipes for MDA, Ecstasy, and Other Psychedelic Amphetamines*. The author writes under the pseudonym "Uncle Fester." Since it first appeared, Uncle Fester's "do it yourself" meth manual has gone through a number of editions.

Uncle Fester's recipe for making methamphetamine includes such skull-and-bones ingredients as hydrochloric acid, lead acetate, drain cleaner (Drano), battery acid and pool acid, lye, lithium batteries, lantern fuel, liquid fertilizer, iodine, lighter fluid, anhydrous ammonia, ether, sodium cyanide, acetone, red phosphorus, and antifreeze. Over-the-counter nasal decongestants and allergy medications such pseudoephedrine (brand names: Sudafed and Claritin) and phenylpropanolamine also make up this dangerous brew.

Ammonia and ether cause the nasty smell manufacturing meth produces. Ammonia is a "deadly respiratory hazard," according to an FBI report in 2000, and sodium metal, another meth ingredient, has the bizarre property of igniting when mixed with water. Sodium cyanide can turn into deadly hydrogen cyanide gas when added to some of the other ingredients that comprise meth, the FBI bulletin reported. Another ingredient, lead acetate, can itself cause death. The National Institute on Drug Abuse has reported that "production errors…may result in methamphetamine contaminated with lead." The user who buys a bad batch of crystal can suffer fatal lead poisoning, especially when the drug is ingested.

You don't have to buy Uncle Fester's cookbook to brew your own crystal at home. KCI: The Anti-Meth Site notes that on the Internet there are "literally thousands" of free recipes and information about manufacturing methamphetamine and other drugs. Making crystal meth is quick and easy: MethAbuse.net says that one batch usually takes only six hours to brew. According to Missouri prosecutor and antidrug expert Cynthia Rushefsky, making meth is "as easy as making a batch of cookies."

"Methamphetamine dealers exchange recipes like you and I would a cookie recipe," says Sgt. Mark Nicastle of the North Metro Drug Task Force in Adams County, Colorado. And you don't have to be a genius to make the drug. The FBI says that less than 10% of people arrested for brewing meth are trained chemists. And while some get the recipe for meth off the Internet, the FBI says others learn the craft from experienced meth makers. Cynthia Rushefsky estimates that each meth cook teaches his or her craft to at least 10 novices.

Still, meth users are a tight-knit fraternity. The National Institute of Justice reports that most users have never purchased the drug from someone they didn't know. In fact, many meth manufacturers are also users who make meth in small quantities for themselves and a small circle of friends.

In 2000, Congress introduced the Methamphetamine and Club Drug Anti-Proliferation Act, which provided for the allocation of $40 million for crystal meth treatment and prevention and made it harder to buy the ingredients used in making crystal. One provision in the bill would have made it illegal to post or exchange crystal recipes on the Internet—but Uncle Fester and other meth mavens need not worry. The American Civil Liberties Union successfully fought to have the provision removed because it "didn't require that a crime be committed before you go to jail," according to ACLU attorney Marv Johnson. "They were criminalizing speech," Johnson explains.

Also, a group of legislators voted to delete the provision because, as former Representative Bob Barr (R-Georgia) and Representative Tammy Baldwin (D-Wisconsin) explained in a press conference, banning Internet recipes for making drugs would start Congress down the "slippery slope" of regulating speech.

The revised proposal passed both the House and Senate and was codified, along with several other drug antiproliferation provisions, as part of The Children's Health Act of 2000. Despite the stringency of the legislation, fighting meth manufacture has remained an uphill battle for law enforcement officers. In testimony before the House Subcommittee on Criminal Justice, Drug Policy, and Human Resources on July 18, 2003, Rogelio Guevara, Chief of Operations for the U.S. Drug Enforcement Administration, said, "Unlike more traditional drugs of abuse like heroin, cocaine, and marijuana, methamphetamine presents some unique challenges. First, it's synthetic, relying on no harvested crops for its manufacture. And, unfortunately, its recipe is relatively easy; anyone who can read and measure can make methamphetamine."

More Bang for Your Buck

There's a good reason why meth labs have so many eager students: No matter how much you put into your lab, you will make a profit. An investment of only $300 can turn into $4,000 worth of crystal after it's been "stepped on"— i.e., diluted with other ingredients. Because selling the drug is so lucrative, "addicts are working just as hard as Dow Chemical," says Colorado drug treatment expert Eugene Strauber.

An investment of a few hundred dollars in over-the-counter drugs and poisonous chemicals is all that is needed to become a part of this genuine cottage industry. The return on investment can amount to thousands of dollars, notes KCI: The Anti-Meth Site. The technology involved in manufacturing crystal meth is so primitive and simple that an entire crystal "lab" can fit in a suitcase. The manufacturing of meth takes up so little room, some labs operate out of cars; this helps them elude police detection, since they are a constantly moving target, or as MethAbuse.net calls them, "rolling labs."

Hotel rooms are also popular sites for meth labs—and

not just in seedy motels, as you might imagine, but in chain hotels catering to businesspeople too.

On May 7, 2004, the Associated Press reported on a flash fire that occurred in a business-class hotel room in Evansville, Indiana: "Reed Skelton was kicking it back on a Saturday night...sipping beer and watching porn when the methamphetamine he was brewing in the bathroom exploded." The explosion resulted in the evacuation of 156 guests and about $120,000 in damage to the hotel.

The same AP report noted the infiltration of meth labs in recent years from the West Coast and Southwest to Heartland states such as Indiana and Kentucky. Hotels are "perfect for 'meth cooks' on the go, even if they're locals." They often check in with stolen identification or pay someone to use their I.D., according to Armand McClintock, who oversees the Indianapolis office of the Drug Enforcement Administration.

In 2003, authorities confiscated 1,260 labs in Indiana, compared with six labs in 1995. Of the 1,260, 17 were found in hotels or motels, Sgt. Todd Ringle of the Indiana State Police told the Associated Press.

In 2003, 309 of the 10,305 meth labs reported to the DEA were in hotel and motel rooms, according to the agency's El Paso Intelligence Center. The national numbers are incomplete because not all labs are reported to the DEA—it's estimated that number would triple if arrests by local authorities were included. Nevertheless, the number of known labs still represents a dramatic increase from 1980, when the DEA seized 251 labs. By 1999, lab seizures had skyrocketed to 2,000, almost 10 times the 1980 number. And from 2,000 in 1999 to 10,305 in 2003: That's 2,000 new labs per year, or 6,000 if one includes the estimated number of local labs.

At this rate, the United States will be looking at more than 52,000 meth labs by 2010—and that figures represents the estimate just for the estimated number of labs seized by authorities.

Cold War

Making meth is easier than in the past, when biker gangs controlled the process and used the solvent phenyl-2-propanone (P2P) as the drug's base. P2P meth involved a complex manufacturing process that was highly volatile and required bulky equipment and a large cooking area. Biker gangs supplied security for these large and sophisticated operations. But in 1980 access to P2P became severely restricted, and the biker-manufacturers went out of business.

Now, the small labs have been so productive in manufacturing meth that many pharmacies in California ration the over-the-counter nasal decongestant Sudafed, one of the ingredients in meth. Also, the federal government prohibits the purchasing of more than eight boxes at a time, even though Sudafed isn't a prescription drug, much less a controlled substance. To counter the restriction, drug shoppers go from store to store, buying their eight-box allotment at various pharmacies.

In 1997, New Jersey-based Warner-Lambert (which has since become part of the drug multinational Pfizer) stopped selling Sudafed and phenylpropanolamine in bottles and began offering them only in individually wrapped blister packets. The intent was to make the manufacturing process more labor-intensive for would-be meth producers.

Shortly after instituting this change, Warner-Lambert

launched a campaign to train sales clerks in pharmacies to spot unusually large purchases of cold and allergy medications containing Sudafed, phenylpropanolamine, pseudoephedrine, and/or ephedrine. Various retailers have since voluntarily agreed to limit the amount of these medications sold to individual customers at one time; early on in 1997, Wal-Mart joined the fight.

As local governments fought meth production, state legislatures throughout the country began to criminalize possession of the drug's ingredients. In 1999, California became the first state to make it a felony to distribute large amounts of pseudoephedrine. In 2001, the Arkansas legislature made possession of more than 12 grams of pseudoephedrine or ephedrine a crime and limited the amount that could be bought at one time to nine grams. That same year, the Washington state legislature enacted a bill that also limited the purchase of pseudoephedrine, ephedrine, and phenylpropanolamine to nine grams per transaction. Also in 2001, Nebraska outlawed the purchase of more than six grams of the three drugs.

The Indiana Drug Enforcement Association—a consortium for federal, state, and local narcotics officers in Indiana—tried a different method. Gary Ashenfelter, a DEA agent in Indiana, explains: "Most [pharmacy clerks], unfortunately, don't know anything about how methamphetamine is made." To educate the clerks and stop the sale of large amounts of the over-the-counter drugs that make up methamphetamine, Indiana began posting a list of these chemicals in pharmacies across the state, with the hope that store clerks would report large-scale purchases of these drugs. Even coffee filters were on the list.

In 2002, the California Department of Alcoholic Beverage Control revoked the liquor license of an establishment in

Escondido for selling large amounts of Sudafed. The owners, Bilial M. Badrani and Haitham H. Mikha, were convicted of this felony and sentenced to 33 months and 21 months, respectively. Badrani and Mikha appealed the liquor license revocation, which the California Department of Alcoholic Beverage Control is allowed to do for "crimes of moral turpitude," but both a judge and the California Department of Alcoholic Beverage Control Appeals Board upheld it. In its decision to confirm the revocation, the Appeals Board said, "The evils associated with methamphetamine are well-documented. Numerous social problems have resulted from its unlawful manufacture, sale, and use. Those who break the law by knowingly supplying essential components of the end product are aiding and abetting in the destruction of society."

These ingredient regulation laws have worked—to some extent. In Congressional testimony, the DEA's Rogelio Guevara said, "The decrease in purity [of methamphetamine] is partially attributed to...chemical control efforts that reduced the supply of those chemicals needed to produce high-quality methamphetamine." Meth manufacturers who try to buy ingredients abroad have also been thwarted. Guevara reported that between March 21 and April 24, 2003, in excess of 22 million pseudoephedrine tablets were seized in Panama and Laredo, Texas. "The tablets were manufactured in Hong Kong and destined for Mexico, where drug traffickers took over the U.S. market from biker gangs around 1994," Guevara said. Even so, Guevara conceded that 95% of meth seized came from small startup operations, not Mexican drug lords.

But there's still a lot of Sudafed out there ready to be converted into lucrative meth. In 2003, in conjunction with the Royal Canadian Mounted Police, the DEA seized almost 50 tons of pseudoephedrine and $17.4 million in cash and made more than 370 arrests in Canada.

Meth Is the New...Meth

Crystal is the roller coaster of illicit drugs—its popularity peaking and waning with no single factor explaining why it falls in and out of fashion. In 1996, the National Household Survey on Drug Abuse (NHSDA) estimated that 4.9 million people (2.3% of the population) have tried methamphetamine at least once.

Use of the drug decreased during the 1994-to-1996 time frame studied by the Drug Abuse Warning Network (DAWN), which surveyed 21 cities and tallied emergency room admissions in which methamphetamine use was suspected. DAWN found that crystal-related admissions to hospitals decreased by 39% between 1994 and 1996. The decline was attributed to the temporary unavailability of the drug. This turned out to be a grace period, since between 1990 and 1994 crystal abuse had jumped 237%. DAWN also found that the number of emergency-room admissions jumped again to 17,000 in 1997—over three times the 4,900 admissions in 1991.

Although methamphetamine is produced locally in makeshift labs across the country, the U.S. trade has been dominated by organized-crime families in the Mexican state of Michoacan since 1992. Within two years of the Mexican takeover, deaths from methamphetamine use in Los Angeles tripled, from 68 fatalities in 1992 to 219 in 1994.

In 1997, NIDA reported that Hawaii, San Francisco, Denver, and Los Angeles were the epicenters of the crisis, although crystal use was then already spreading to other

areas. California has become the Goliath of meth manufacturing, with an estimated 80% of the nation's supply
coming from the state. The number of illegal labs found in
California tripled between 1995 and 2000. More than 95%
of the large-scale labs seized by authorities in 1999 were in
California, as were 400 smaller ones. (The DEA defines
large-scale labs as facilities able to produce more than 20
pounds of meth in one batch.) In total, the DEA confiscated 2,001 labs in California in 1999, as compared with
only two labs in New Jersey, one in New York, and none in
Massachusetts, Connecticut, Vermont, Maine, Delaware,
or Rhode Island.

Until 1995, when labs began to pop up in the Midwest
and Southeast, meth remained largely a California phenomenon. In Missouri, police busted just two labs in 1992, but by
1998 that number had jumped to 600. Some Iowa police
departments report that meth-related arrests outnumber
DUIs. DAWN says that meth-related emergency room
admissions rose from 4,900 in 1991 to 17,000 in 1997. In
August 2004, *The Chattanoogan* reported that "The U.S.
Drug Enforcement Administration estimates that Tennessee
now accounts for 75% of meth lab seizures in the Southeast."
And in January 2004 an opinion piece in *The Honolulu
Advertiser* pointed out that Hawaii has been suffering an
epidemic of "smoking ice" since 1989. The editorial
bemoaned both the lack of state funding for meth rehabilitation and the drug's easy accessibility in Hawaii prisons.

Just because few meth labs have been found in New
York state does not mean that use of the drug is not on the
upswing there. In January 2004, *The New York Times*
reported that almost two dozen 12-step meetings for meth
addicts are held each week in New York City. Two years
earlier, there had been only four Crystal Meth Anonymous

meetings each week—and as recently as 1999 there had been none. "Just a few years ago, we were worrying about the arrival of crystal meth," Perry N. Halkitis, a psychologist at New York University, told *The New York Times.* "Well, it's finally here."

Halkitis predicts that "it's just a matter of time" before crystal use in urban areas will become mainstream—that is, not just a drug used by gay men. After all, *The Times* attests, in the nation's heartland crystal has become symptomatic of rural decline.

But New York's public health officials—as well as its gay groups—seem to be in denial about the city's emerging meth epidemic. In 2004, ACT UP's Peter Staley took matters into his own hands with a controversial ad campaign. The ads read "Buy crystal, get HIV free!" and were plastered on Verizon phone booths. Staley paid for them with $6,000 of his own money.

A recovering crystal addict himself, Staley told *The Times,* "My goal is to get the drug the reputation it deserves. My fear is that young gay men think it's the latest party drug. I want crystal to get the stigma that heroin has. It is not glamorous; it is not alluring."

Staley says his problem originated in the all-night dance clubs where crystal use runs rampant. "I've tried every drug in the book and never got addicted, but this one grabbed me by the throat the first time I did it," said Staley. "I'm a control freak. I mean, I couldn't get addicted to cigarettes, but I couldn't give crystal up."

⸿ • In San Francisco—where, according to SFGate.com, it is estimated that up to 40% of gay men have tried crystal and where 76% of the primary meth hospital admissions in 1997 were men—public health officials allocated $425,000 in 2003 to fight the drug. Area groups working to curb gay and bisexual men away from the drug and, hopefully, away from HIV infection. The bulk of the funds ($250,000) went to programs working with young gay, bisexual, and transgender men and women—in an effort to lead them away from meth and in so doing away from HIV—while $100,000 went to the Stonewall Project, a counseling service for gay and bisexual meth users.

The fight against crystal meth is taking shape elsewhere in the United States too. In April 2004, the *Lexington* (Kentucky) *Herald-Leader* reported that the city of Lexington was considering a law that would allow health officials and the medical licensure board to use a database to track suspicious prescription patterns; meanwhile, *The Herald-Palladium* in Case County, Michigan, said citizens would consider a tax hike to fund anti-meth efforts. Even *The Algona–Upper Des Moines,* a small-town newspaper in northern Iowa, reported that as the end of the 2003-2004 academic year approached, guidance counselors in the local school system prepped teens for summer vacation by informing them of the hazards of meth.

Stay-at-Home Mom-and-Pop

Like moonshiners during Prohibition, many of today's crystal manufacturers are mom-and-pop operations run by undocumented workers who find making meth much more lucrative than stoop labor. Meth labs are small and portable, and they commonly make use of everyday items like plastic tubing and soft-drink bottles.

"A clandestine lab operator can utilize relatively common items such as mason jars, coffee filters, hot plates, pressure cookers, pillowcases, gas cans, etc., to substitute for sophisticated laboratory equipment," DEA chief Rogelio

Guevara said during Congressional testimony in July 2003. Ironically, the decline in the purity of crystal sold may be good news for drug users. "Decreasing purity levels for methamphetamine...should have some [positive] effect on the number of emergency room admissions and overdose deaths related to methamphetamine," Guevara added.

Meth labs are often located in abandoned barns and shacks in remote rural area. The FBI reports that several urban apartment complexes and even a luxury hotel that were doing double duty as meth labs have burned to the ground. The Knight Ridder/Tribune News Service has asserted that labs in the boondocks have destroyed the "Mayberry-like ambience in large chunks" of small-town and rural America.

꙰ Authorities have tackled the onslaught of meth labs with increased training—of their own staff and that of local motels and hotels. The Associated Press has reported that officers from the Evansville-Vanderburgh Joint Narcotics Task Force have met individually with area hotel owners and managers to teach them what to look for—the smell of anhydrous ammonia, which is used to make the drug; the repeated appearance of suspicious-seeming locals—as well as how to respond if they find a meth lab. Across the Ohio River from Evansville, the Kentucky State Police addressed the same topic at an annual meeting of the Kentucky Hotel and Lodging Association.

Some meth lab operators in remote areas are so brazen that they cook their product outdoors to escape the toxic fumes that arise during the manufacturing process. The fumes, which one law enforcement official described as smelling like a combination of battery acid and rotten eggs, can act like a homing beacon for government drug busters. To neutralize the incriminating smell, operators use a hose to filter the fumes through kitty litter, venting the sanitized fumes outdoors. This filtering process works best with small-time production of meth; larger manufacturers prefer to concoct their product outside, where the smell is more easily dissipated than indoors.

Because of its many remote areas, the American Southwest has become a popular manufacturing center of methamphetamine. To hide the odor, some meth manufacturers burn trash while they brew. Thus, the smell of burning trash has also become a beacon for police.

There Goes the Neighborhood

"You can make crystal at home out of ingredients that are available anywhere," says UCLA's Edwin Bayrd. However, he adds, "One dangerous step involves cooking it, and your lab can blow up."

A rave review by one of the buyers of Uncle Fester's methamphetamine cookbook is posted on Amazon.com and echoes Bayrd's caveat: "Uncle Fester tells you several techniques, step-by-step, exactly how to make meth. But it's kind of like someone telling you step-by-step how to make nitroglycerine. It's one of those things you don't want to just read about and then take a shot at. If you don't for sure know exactly what you're doing, you'll probably find yourself in the center of a violent ball of flame when your experiment blows up in your face." Red phosphorus, one of the ingredients in crystal, is what makes matchsticks ignite. The chemical, which is highly flammable, is also used in road flares.

' Besides the toll the drug takes on its producers and users, innocent bystanders can also be harmed by its major biohazards. Of the approximately 32 ingredients that go into making methamphetamine, one third are "extremely toxic," according to the January 2001 issue of *Sierra* magazine. Some of the ingredients are also explosive, flammable, and corrosive. Of the more than 1,600 illegal labs shut down in 1998, 20% first came to the attention of authorities because they exploded or burned down. And, for every pound of crystal produced, five or six pounds of toxic waste are also created.

In a 1997 press conference to announce the launch of the DEA's anti-methamphetamine program called Operation Meta, former U.S. Attorney General Janet Reno emphasized the toxic consequences of making meth: "To anyone who has forgotten about the dangers posed by methamphetamine, consider this. In Los Angeles, Operation Meta had dismantled three meth labs. One operated just a few yards away from a day care center and two schools. And the fleeing traffickers left 15 gallons of toxic and volatile chemicals still cooking." Reno promised, "We aren't going to let methamphetamine spread across America the way crack did in the 1980s."

Too late.

An article in the April 2000 issue of *The FBI Law Enforcement Bulletin* notes that local police are often out of their depth when it comes to seizing labs. "Today, encountering hazardous chemicals remains no less dangerous than pursuing an armed suspect. Very few officers have expertise in firefighting, chemistry, bomb-handling techniques, and hazardous waste disposal. Unfortunately, illegal drug laboratories pose deadly threats in all of these areas." Besides harboring lethal chemicals, some labs have mechanical and chemical booby traps installed by lab operators.

Meth manufacturers themselves are at even greater risk

for hazardous-materials exposure than law enforcement officials. In 1995, defective gas masks were found near the corpses of undocumented meth lab workers in remote areas of Central and Southern California. In 2000, two meth manufacturers died after inhaling phosphene fumes. Four police officers who raided the lab were also overcome by the fumes and had to be hospitalized. Indeed, since 1995, the FBI reports that on average three meth makers per year have been killed in explosions or by toxic chemicals while concocting their potions, and many other manufacturers suffer severe burns and other injuries from lab fires. And NIDA considers that a department of the National Institutes of Health, says "acute lead poisoning is a potential risk" for both the makers and users of crystal because "production errors may result in methamphetamine contaminated with lead."

The Iceman Spilleth

Cleanup of seized meth labs and meth lab fires resembles something out of a sci-fi or disaster film. In order to gather evidence for prosecution, police officers have to don hermetically sealed "moon suits with self-contained breathing apparatus," reported *Sierra* in 2001. The same article also quoted Lt. Andrew Tafoya, a law enforcement officer in St. Johns, Arizona, on meth lab cleanup: "I would rather investigate a homicide than a meth lab. These labs are a logistical and environmental nightmare."

The reaction between red phosphorus and iodine, two of the ingredients in meth, can create a lethal gas, phosphene, which has the added danger of being odorless. "If we don't know it's a lab when we go in, the immediate danger is that we don't have breathing apparatuses on and we inhale toxic gasses that can kill us or fry our lungs," Tafoya said.

After the police perform the dangerous task of collecting evidence from a meth lab, hazmat (hazardous materials) teams have to be called in to clean up the mess. Cleanup, besides being dangerous, is also very pricey. It can cost up to $100,000 to decontaminate a large site and $3,000 to $4,000 for smaller labs.

Some sites are impossible to detoxify no matter how much money is spent. Chemicals from the manufacturing process can remain embedded in walls, carpets, plaster, and the wood used to fuel meth factories. The dumps can remain so toxic that government authorities often decline to confiscate the properties because they fear liability lawsuits by anyone fearless or reckless enough to buy the confiscated land.

Meth manufacturers often pour the by-products of their poisonous stew down storm drains or dump it on the ground, where it can seep into the water table. Other producers brazenly run a pipe from their labs to nearby streams to get rid of leftover chemicals. And perhaps most shocking of all, some pour the toxic by-products down wells. The discarded chemicals create a long-lasting environmental disaster as the residue from crystal manufacture often remains in the soil and water table for years. "It's toxic waste. We find holes dug where they've buried the stuff for weeks on end. The liquid eats into the ground, or they pipe it right into the creeks," says Officer Moise Reyes of the San Jose Police Department, who also acts as liaison to the Bureau of Narcotic Enforcement of the California Department of Justice. Meth lab residue is so toxic that the only safe—and extremely costly—way to remove it is to burn the leftover drugs.

-6-

Speed Traps: Meth and the Law

"THE MOST COMMONLY REPORTED REASON WHY METHAMPHETAMINE USERS ENTER TREATMENT IS TROUBLE WITH THE LAW."
—NATIONAL INSTITUTE ON DRUG ABUSE

"A FRIEND OF MINE INTRODUCED IT TO ME, AND I TRIED IT OUT OF CURIOSITY. I PLUNGED INTO THE WORLD OF ILLICIT USE AND MANUFACTURING OF METH HEAD-ON.... IT LANDED ME IN PRISON TWICE, ONCE FOR A YEAR AND ONCE FOR FOUR YEARS."
—SHANE

"I WAS A 16-YEAR-OLD FOOTBALL PLAYER WHO STARTED USING TO PULL CRAM SESSIONS FOR TESTS AND EXAMS. I ALWAYS THOUGHT THAT I WOULD BE ABLE TO KEEP IT UNDER CONTROL. SINCE THEN I'VE LOST MY HEALTH, SPENT A YEAR IN JAIL, AND LOST MY CREDIBILITY."
—JEREMY

It's not just their health that crystal users are risking when they ingest the drug. There can be severe legal consequences as well. A Google search of the Internet for "methamphetamine" produces 12,000 Web sites devoted to the topic. Yahoo hosts 214,000 sites! And ominously, one of the more frequently visited sites devoted to crystal is entitled Criminal Defense; it offers "free, immediate consultation with one of our criminal defense lawyers with over 30 years of experience covering crimes and legal charges such as sex, drugs, violent, and white-collar offenses."

In November 2000, California voters approved a ballot initiative called Proposition 36, which diverts first-time and second-time nonviolent offenders convicted of drug possession to rehab facilities instead of prison. A thrifty decision: Drug rehabilitation programs cost about one tenth of the expense of incarcerating drug offenders, according to the NIDA.

The UCLA Integrated Substance Abuse Program tracked the impact of Proposition 36 during its first year of enforcement in 2001. The study found that 50% of the 30,000 people sent to rehab instead of prison that year were methamphetamine users. Cocaine users diverted to rehab came in a distant second at 15%, marijuana users made up 12% of those diverted, and heroin users represented 11% of the group. Of those individuals diverted from prison to rehab, 50% were white, 31% were Latino, and 14% were black.

John Duran, a criminal defense attorney in West Hollywood, describes the legal consequences of methamphetamine use in California. A first-time arrest is what Duran calls "a divertible offense. If the defendant doesn't have a prior record, he is sentenced to a four-month drug rehab program." If the defendant has a prior criminal record, he may be eligible for treatment called "drug court," in which the defendant is closely supervised by a judge, who determines the length of treatment, with a cap of three years. "It's up to the judge to decide when to cut you loose," Duran says. If the defendant has multiple arrests for drug offenses, he or she could face a maximum of three years in prison in California.

Drug dealers aren't allowed to participate in drug diversion programs in lieu of prison time. The quantity of drugs that distinguishes a drug user from a drug dealer is "a subjective call and only one of the components" that defines dealing, Duran says. Possession of a large amount of crystal may not necessarily mean you're selling the drug. "It may just mean that you have a major drug habit," Duran says.

Another component that helps distinguish between using and dealing is whether one possesses the tools of the trade: scales to weigh the drug, plastic baggies for distributing it, other packaging materials, lots of cash present, and something Duran calls "buy-and-sell sheets," which record drug transactions.

A Drug Court Grad

Someone who calls himself "Bigmoy" on the KCI message board says it took a car crash and time in jail before he sought the help of a 12-step program.

Bigmoy is 42, and he says he used crystal for 22 years. In the beginning, he had the typical honeymoon with the drug. After four stints in jail and the loss of 18 jobs, he admits that his life had become unmanageable—a realization that is supposed to occur in the first of the 12 steps.

Everything became clear when he was high on crystal and driving 70 mph with his nephew in the passenger seat. He decided to make a U-turn without slowing down and crashed into a parked semitrailer. Fortunately, the car slid under the semi-trailer and no one was hurt. But when the police arrived, they discovered Bigmoy had a packet of crystal in his pocket. He was also drunk, so the police booked him on drug possession and a felony DUI.

After four months in jail, he was offered the choice of going to state prison or attending drug court and having his behavior closely monitored by a judge. Choosing the latter, Bigmoy completed the 18-month drug court program, then returned to school and earned a certificate in human services for drug and alcohol counseling. He says he is about three classes away from earning a two-year college degree.

These days, the once-unemployable drug addict has found a dream job as a drug counselor in Porterville, California. "My life is getting better every day, thanks to Drug Court and Narcotics Anonymous and Alcoholics Anonymous. The most important person in my life, God, has given me the strength to make positive choices in my life today."

A Second Chance

Federal penalties for possession of crystal are much less ambiguous and more severe than California's; it doesn't take too much of the drug to bump the user into the more legally liable terrain of "trafficker." Possession of 10 grams or $800 worth of the drug automatically qualifies the user as a trafficker or retailer, and the minimum mandatory federal sentence for 10 grams is five years in prison. Possession of 100 grams will put you away for 10 years.

Crystal is so ubiquitous and is used so openly at bathhouses, sex clubs, and circuit parties that people often forget or are too disoriented by the drug to remember that there are criminal penalties for using it.

"The most commonly reported reason why methamphetamine users enter treatment is trouble with the law," states the NIDA's Web site. "These legal problems include aggressive or bizarre behaviors, which prompt others to call the police."

Legal problems—as well as a good, hard look at what he'd become—motivated drug treatment specialist Cary Quashen to seek help 23 years ago. He hasn't used since. "I resisted getting treatment at first. Nobody wakes up and decides they want to get clean and sober," Quashen says. Negative fallout from drug use is a prime motivator in seeking help. "The consequences of what [drug users] are doing has to outweigh the fun they think they're having."

Some of the consequences Quashen lists include a lover who leaves the addict because of drug use, trouble at work, and medical problems "so bad [that users] don't know what to do." Quashen's personal bottom occurred when "I got tired of waking up and not liking what I had turned into."

-7-
The Life and Death of the Party

"On Ecstasy, I'll make out with a troll...or even a girl."
— gay porn star Christian River Wolf

"In the beginning, crystal is a wonderful drug to dance on. You can get the feeling that the party is never going to end on crystal."
— Richard

"Crank at first seemed to speed up everything in my life, but now looking back it has slowed down all of the rewarding experiences needed to live a normal happy life."
— Kristina

A tour of Internet Web sites reveals that for some people, the party isn't confined to weekends.

It's Wednesday, the middle of the work day, and 36 America Online subscribers have squeezed into Los Angeles–San Diego chat room of M4M (Men for Men), a Web site with chat rooms and personals that is the Internet equivalent of a gay pickup bar. Four of the room's visitors explicitly allude to drug use in their e-mail handles: Sxy30sPNPDude, PnPhotplay, WLAPnPLean29, and Partyin Naked. "Party" is a euphemism for using meth, "play" refers to sex, and "PnP" is an abbreviation of the combination of the two: "party and play," i.e., having sex while high on crystal.

Several other men in the chat room have "party" listed as a hobby in their online autobiographical profiles. And many of the chat room's inhabitants write that they're "tweaking," which either means they're flying high on crystal or they're coming down from it, also known as "crashing."

Crystal is only one of several psychostimulants or psychoactive drugs that are popular among the gay party-and-play crowd of both gay and heterosexual ravers. Raves are dance events that originated in the mid 1980s as secret gathering places for young, gay Brits. Since alcohol wasn't sold, personal identification didn't need to be checked, and raves soon became popular gatherings for the under-21 set.

Cocaine, GHB, Ecstasy (MDMA), ketamine (also known as "Vitamin K"), PCP ("angel dust"), Rohypnol ("the date-rape drug"), and LSD also figure into partying. Despite their different chemical compositions, every stimulant listed except LSD has the same intoxicating mechanism to flood the brain with pleasure-enhancing chemicals.

The Caviar of Drugs

Cocaine mimics many of the effects of methamphetamine. The prohibitive cost of cocaine and the speed with which it leaves the body, however, make it less popular than crystal. One of the reasons methamphetamine is so much cheaper than cocaine is that meth is produced domestically and doesn't have to be transported across international borders tightened by post–9/11 security measures.[5] One quarter of a gram of crystal costs $20 to $60, slightly higher than a similar amount of cocaine, according to CrystalRecovery.com, but the fact that crystal's effects last so much longer has made it the poor man's cocaine.

While smoking crystal creates a high that can last up to 24 hours, the high from smoking cocaine lasts less than 10 minutes, and 50% of the drug—called a "half life"—leaves the body after only one hour. Crystal's half life is 12 hours. The high from snorting cocaine is even shorter, lasting only minutes, hence the need for repeated use. Coke users at parties are notorious for becoming agitated and disappearing into a bathroom, from which they emerge elated— definitely not stressed out anymore.

Despite the drug's high cost and minimal effect, Alan I. Leshner, former director of the National Institute on Drug Abuse, says that cocaine use, like crystal use, has reached epidemic proportions. "Cocaine abuse and addiction continue to be a problem that plagues our nation. In 1997, for example, an estimated 1.5 million Americans age 12 and older were chronic cocaine abusers. Although this is an improvement over the 1985 estimate of 5.7 million users, we still have a substantial distance to go in reducing the use of this addictive stimulant." In 2003, the National Household Survey on Drug Abuse (NHSDA) reported that 3.6 million Americans were chronic cocaine users.

Cocaine is an alkaloid derived from the Peruvian and Bolivian coca plant. For more than a thousand years, the native peoples of South America have chewed coca leaves to banish fatigue and fend off the cold. Chewing coca leaves is a mild stimulant. Cocaine hydrochloride, the powdered form sold today, was first extracted from the leaves of the erythroxylon coca bush in South America 150 years ago. Powdered cocaine is much more intoxicating than the leaves of its parent plant.

By the beginning of the 20th century, cocaine was promoted as a wonder drug and became the active ingredient in many patent medicines used to treat a variety of ailments. Before he became addicted to the drug and went through painful withdrawal, Sigmund Freud believed cocaine had the potential to become a cure-all.

The Drug Enforcement Administration (DEA) has classified cocaine as a Schedule II drug—just like crystal—and this classification means that a drug has serious potential for abuse. Cocaine comes in two forms: cocaine hydrochloride, a white, crystalline powder; and crack, also known as freebase. In powder form, cocaine hydrochloride can be snorted or dissolved in water and injected intravenously. Powdered cocaine is often diluted by dealers with inert ingredients like cornstarch, talcum powder, sugar, or baby laxative and with active drugs like the local anesthetic procaine. This form of cocaine is also sometimes cut with amphetamine, which increases the amount of the drug available for sale and gives cocaine amphetamine's more powerful (and cheaper) high.

Crack or freebase cocaine is derived from cocaine hydrochloride. It's produced by adding ammonia or baking soda and water to cocaine hydrochloride. The mixture is then heated to remove hydrochloride. The drug's name comes from the crackling sound it makes when smoked.

The NHSDA says crack cocaine use remains an intractable problem in the United States and estimates that 604,000 Americans use it regularly. Crack cocaine use spans the age spectrum. In 1998, NIDA's Monitoring the Future Survey reported the starling statistic that the percentage of eighth graders who have used crack at least once is 3.2%, a rise from 1997's 2.7%.

The typical crack smoker feels a rush of euphoria within 10 seconds after smoking it, followed by a less intoxicating high that lasts only five to 10 minutes. (The high from snorting takes longer to occur, but lasts up to 30 minutes.) The high from crack is so intensely pleasurable; smokers typically find themselves using more crack after the first five or 10 minutes of bliss wear off.

According to NIDA the popularity of crack is due to the speed and intensity with which it takes effect. Another reason for the drug's popularity is its cheapness. A single "rock" of crack cocaine costs only $10, but the short duration of the high prompts the user to smoke more, and crack can end up costing much more than longer-lasting crystal during a typical "run" or binge.

The stereotype of crack as a drug for the poor and underprivileged is just that. Take Michelle, a Ph.D. candidate who has let the drug devastate her economically and put her impressive career on hold. Michelle is what is known as an "ABD" ("all but dissertation"), which means she has finished her university course work; all that's left for her to complete is her doctoral dissertation.

Crack has put Michelle's dissertation on hold indefinitely as she chronically relapses and has trouble achieving 30 days of continuous sobriety. During brief periods off the drug, the doctoral candidate works as a waitress. Since her dealer is also a fence, Michelle pays for her ever-increasing use of the drug by barter—giving the dealer her personal possessions, including her stereo and her BMW, in return for crack. "You just hand over everything you own," she says.

Crack is also an extremely physically dangerous drug. The Drug Abuse Warning Network (DAWN) reported a 78% increase between 1990 and 1994 in crack cocaine-related admissions to emergency rooms nationwide. In 1996, there were 152,433 E.R. visits due to complications from crack use.

NIDA states that there is no safe way to use any form of cocaine. Binges can put toxic amounts of the drug in the bloodstream and excessive use can lead to heart attacks and strokes. In small doses of 100 milligrams or less, cocaine, like crystal, produces euphoria, energy, and increased alertness. Some say the drug allows them to focus more, while others feel scattered and incapable of completing simple tasks. Users quickly develop a tolerance to cocaine and find themselves having to use more of the drug to recreate their first high—another case of chasing the uncatchable dragon.

The short-term effects of moderate cocaine use (100 milligrams or less) are fairly benign: constricted blood vessels, dilated pupils, and elevated blood temperature (hyperthermia), heart rate, and blood pressure. Binges on several hundred milligrams can lead to violent and unpredictable behavior. Large amounts of the drug can cause tremors, vertigo, muscle twitches, and paranoia; low doses of cocaine can cause restlessness, anxiety, and irritability.

Sometimes, although rarely, sudden death can occur the first time the drug is ingested. The most frequent causes of death from cocaine are heart attacks, seizures, and respiratory arrest. The drug can also cause arrhythmia (irregular heartbeat), chest pains, abdominal pain, headaches, and gastrointestinal diseases such as irritable bowel syndrome and nausea. The long-term effects of cocaine use can cause the same auditory hallucinations that plague crystal users. Binges can create full-blown paranoid psychosis.

Because cocaine acts as an appetite suppressant, users may experience dramatic weight-loss and malnutrition. IV-users can contract HIV and hepatitis A, B, and C by sharing contaminated needles. Between 65 and 90% of IV-users of cocaine are infected with the hepatitis C virus.

There's currently no drug available to treat cocaine addiction. Antidepressants have been somewhat helpful in counteracting the mood swings typical of chronic users.

Two drugs, Selegiline and Disulfiram, are in various stages of clinical trials. Disulfiram has been effective in treating alcoholism. At present, NIDA says the only effective treatment for cocaine addiction is cognitive behavioral therapy, a short-term treatment wherein the users identify and avoid behaviors that trigger cocaine use.

The Belle of the Ball

It's easy to see why the sedative-hypnotic GHB (gamma hydroxybutyrate) is such a popular "party" drug. In small doses (one capful), GHB, which comes in powdered form or as a clear liquid with a very bitter taste, gives users extra energy and increases their desire to socialize, making them feel affectionate and playful. GHB has a disinhibiting effect; it can foster euphoria, heighten sensuality, and dramatically enhance sex.

Amphetamines.com has posted this warning about GHB usage: "At lower doses, GHB can relax the user, but as the dose increases, the sedative effects may result in sleep and eventual coma or death." There are other dangers associated with GHB use. The drug can take up to two hours to take effect, and impatient partygoers may take additional—and deadly—doses while they're waiting for the initial dose to kick in. The high from GHB usually lasts two to three hours, but sometimes the effects of the drug can linger on for 24 hours.

According to the DanceSafe Web site, which promotes health and safety in the rave and nightclub community, a single capful of GHB "can impair motor coordination as much as six drinks of alcohol." Even the so-called recommended dose of one capful can cause loss of consciousness. "It's hard to find the proper dose with GHB. A teaspoon might be perfect once but an overdose the next time. It depends on body weight, how much food is in the stomach, and other random factors," DanceSafe says.

The Project GHB Web site says, "The dosage response of GHB is quite steep, meaning that a tiny increase in dosage may cause a dramatic increase in symptoms and, thus, in risk.

Drinking alcohol or using other depressants while under the influence of GHB increases the risk of overdose and death. Both Project GHB and DanceSafe warn that the drug is highly addictive, and possession can result in long prison terms.

Large doses can cause slurred speech, difficulty concentrating, giddiness, rambling, incoherent speech, nausea, headaches, dizziness, tremor, amnesia, vomiting, loss of muscle control, loss of the gag reflex, (victims can choke to death on their own vomit), hallucinations, bradycardia, (slow heart rate), respiratory arrest, and loss of consciousness (one of the most common effects). Project GHB says most users "sleep off a GHB overdose; those who don't are called *dead*."

Losing consciousness while on the drug has become so common it has generated street names such as "carpeting out," "scooping out," and "throwing down." At circuit parties, at least one GHB user on average passes out, and a common sight at these events is an ambulance parked outside as paramedics try to revive someone lying on the street after being carried off the dance floor unconscious.

Because the drug is colorless in liquid form, sexual predators have been known to spike their victims' drinks with GHB. Project GHB reports that "GHB has become a major cause of drug-related comas in the U.S. and other countries." The site also says that the number of overdoses from the drug now surpass those from Ecstasy.

While Los Angeles journalist Jeffrey was researching GHB for a magazine article, he learned that it can cause respiratory arrest and death. Then, at a circuit party, he saw someone collapse on the dance floor. The staff carried the unconscious man to a couch and just left him there. Jeffrey went over to the couch, and when he noticed the man was not breathing he suspected a GHB overdose. As it turned out, Jeffrey's ex-boyfriend, a physician, was at the circuit party, and Jeffrey dragooned him into performing CPR on the victim while waiting for the paramedics to arrive. "I was amazed at the callousness of the [party] staff," Jeffrey says. "They just left him on the couch to die. If I hadn't been in the middle of researching my article on GHB, I wouldn't have known the drug can cause respiratory arrest, and the guy probably would have died right there on the couch." (The DanceSafe Web site emphasizes this important—but hopefully unnecessary—reminder: "If you're at a rave or nightclub and someone falls unconscious or has a seizure, call an ambulance immediately.")

GHB was discovered in the 1960s in France, where researchers hoped to use it as an anesthetic, but the drug's toxic properties ruled out such use. It was first legally imported into the United States in 1987 as a possible treatment for narcolepsy, but after so many reports of overdoses on the drug, the U.S. government made it illegal in 1990.

After GHB was illegalized, drug dealers began selling legal precursors, or analogs (drugs with similar molecular structure to GHB)—such as GBL (gamma butyrolactone), GHV (gamma hydroxyvalerate), and BD (1,4-butanediol)—which, when ingested, instantly convert to GHB. These analogs were outlawed in March 2000. Still, the Project

GHB site marvels at how "unsettling it is that these pre-cursors…are [readily] available at gyms, chemical supply stores, on the Internet, and through mail order."

One wonders if GHB would still be so popular if people knew of its poisonous ingredients. Like crystal, most of the ingredients have a skull-and-crossbones label and include a degreasing solvent, floor stripper, drain cleaner, nail polish, Super Glue, and lye.

One Internet recipe on how to make GHB carries this warning: "Wear gloves and safety glasses at all times. If any of the [chemicals] contact the skin, wash well with cold water. To store it, I use a mason jar with plastic cover. I draw the poison logo on it."

The X Games

Another wildly popular party drug is Ecstasy, also known as MDMA (3,4-methylenedioxymethampheta-mine). The drug was first synthesized in 1912 by the German pharmaceutical giant Merck, which patented it two years later and hoped to market the drug as an appetite suppressant. In the 1970s, articles began appearing in medical journals praising MDMA as an adjunct to psy-chotherapy. Psychologists gave the drug to patients to make it easier for them to discuss their feelings. Ecstasy was made illegal in 1985 after animal studies showed that it causes damage to the serotoninergic axons in the brain and also damaged the cells that release serotonin. A typical dose ranges between 80 to 150 milligrams, and the price fluctuates wildly from $20 to $50 per pill.

Ecstasy is popular mainly because it promotes empathy, emotional warmth, and openness, a feeling of genuinely communicating with others, a reduction of critical and cynical thoughts—or as "Erowid," a Webmaster who is bullish on the drug, says, "Users are likely to find that everything is right with the world." Many users, however, say that this euphoria only occurs the first time Ecstasy is ingested; users end up unsuccessfully trying to recapture the original high.

Ecstasy works its temporary magic by flooding the brain with the pleasure-enhancing neurotransmitter serotonin, the active ingredient in antidepressants like Prozac. As Ecstasy leaves the body, the brain's naturally produced serotonin remains lowered because of the drug, and this causes depression, which leads some to use more of the drug to alleviate withdrawal symptoms. Another neurotransmitter, dopamine, is also reduced by Ecstasy.

Even while high on the drug, some users suffer headaches, chills, eye twitching, jaw clenching, blurred vision, and nausea, according to the Web site Neuroscience for Kids. The reason this youth-oriented page discusses Ecstasy is because it links with the results from the annual surveys of drug use among eight graders and high school sophomores and seniors done by Monitoring the Future, an ongoing study of youth conducted at the Institute for Social Research at the University of Michigan. Among the 50,000 students surveyed, 2.1% of eighth graders, 3% of sophomores, and 4.5% of high school seniors had used Ecstasy in the past year. Though these figures represent a slight decline from 2000 and 2001 levels, they are still unsettling.

The fact that children are using this drug becomes more disturbing when some of Ecstasy's other negative side effects are identified: confusion, depression, insomnia, hallucinations, severe anxiety, violent and irrational behavior, dehydration, hypertension (high blood pressure), and heart or kidney failure. So much for feeling connected to the world.

According to a Web page entitled "Ecstasy: A Not So Bright Idea," Ecstasy users scored lower than nonusers on three intelligence tests, required more repetitions to learn a word, and their short-term memory was impaired. The unidentified Webmaster of the site observes, "The researchers concluded that MDMA use over a period of months or a few years may cause long-term impairment of cognitive performance, even when MDMA is taken in relatively small doses."

George Ricaurte, an associate professor of neurology at Johns Hopkins University, performed PET-scans on a group of Ecstasy users. Although their behavior appeared normal, the tests revealed dramatic neurological damage. Ricaurte reported a 20%-to-60% reduction in healthy serotonin cells among the users whose brains he scanned. "Damage to these cells could affect a person's abilities to remember and to learn," Ricaurte says.

In the June 15, 1999 issue of *The Journal of Neuroscience,* Ricaurte published a study that compared monkeys who had received Ecstasy dissolved in a liquid twice a day for four days to a control group of monkeys who had received the same liquid without Ecstasy for that same period of time. The monkeys who had been given the Ecstasy-laced liquid experienced damage to the frontal lobes of their cerebral cortices. (Human brains use the frontal lobe for analysis, problem solving, critical thinking, and empathy.) The monkeys' hippocampi, which govern memory, were also damaged. Even worse, the damage to the serotonin-containing nerve cells in the monkeys who had been given Ecstasy was still visible seven years later, if less acute than when it was first measured two weeks after consumption.

Although pure MDMA isn't a hallucinogen, the drug is often diluted with amphetamine, methamphetamine, and the hallucinogens LSD and psilocybin, which explains reports of hallucinating on the drug. To increase their supply, drug dealers also cut MDMA with caffeine and lactose.

The DanceSafe Web site says, "Ecstasy isn't physically addictive. However, the drug can often take on great importance in people's lives, and some...become rather compulsive in their use. Taken too frequently, however, MDMA loses its special effect."

Ecstasy usually kicks in about 20 to 40 minutes after consumption. After 60 to 90 minutes, the user peaks on the drug, and its effect can last three to six hours. The typical dose is 100 to 125 milligrams, and it comes in capsule or tablet form. Also, there's a great deal of counterfeit Ecstasy that sometimes contains little or none of the drug.

Some Other Suspects

Less popular than Ecstasy and GHB are the party drugs ketamine, Rohypnol, PCP, and that 1960s classic LSD, which never seems to fall out of favor. Ketamine was first synthesized for use as an animal anesthetic in 1960. Use of a small amount of ketamine results in loss of attention span. At higher doses, ketamine can cause delirium, amnesia, high blood pressure, depression, and severe breathing problems. "Vitamin K" can also cause memory loss and hurt a person's learning ability.

Rohypnol, the most sinister party drug, has come to be called the "date-rape drug." It's tasteless and odorless—thus, perfect for spiking a stranger's drink. The drug is popular with rapists also because it causes amnesia.

Luckily, at least one potential victim was accidentally
saved when her laced drink also included cranberry juice,
which counteracts the drug. With her memory intact, she
was able to identify her would-be rapist, who was arrested
and charged.

A genuinely poisonous drug is PCP (angel dust),
which was original synthesized as an anesthetic for surgery on animals, especially on primates. Smoking cigaril-
los dipped in PCP and marijuana cigarettes laced with
the drug is a popular way to ingest it. PCP is a toxic drug
that can cause delirium, amnesia, high blood pressure,
depression, anxiety, and severe breathing problems—as
well as psychosis and extreme violent behavior. Overdose
and death are common.

Granddaddy Acid

Finally, there's the granddaddy of psychoactive drugs, d-
Lysergic Acid Diethylamide, better known by its street
names LSD or acid. Besides causing wild and often disturbing hallucinations, the drug, which typically takes 30
to 90 minutes to take effect, also causes side effects such
as numbness, weakness, nausea, increased heart rate,
sweating, lack of appetite, insomnia, terrifying thoughts,
fear of insanity and death, despair, and flashbacks to previous experiences on the drug. These flashbacks can occur
up to a year after the user has stopped taking the drug.

Unlike its chemical cousins, LSD is a serotonin antag-
onist, which means that it blocks the pleasure-causing
neurochemical serotonin, which may explain many a bad
trip on the drug. But NIDA reports that bad "trips" are
only some of the dangers associated with LSD. Chronic
LSD usage may result in "relatively long-lasting psychoses,

such as schizophrenia or severe depression."

Unlike its party cousins, LSD isn't considered physically addictive. NIDA reports that LSD "does not produce compulsive and drug-seeking behavior, [unlike] cocaine, amphetamine, heroin, alcohol, and nicotine." However, many LSD users eventually develop a tolerance to the substance and need to increase their doses to achieve their original high.

LSD is an odorless, colorless, and bitter-tasting liquid, which is often dripped on tiny squares of blotter paper. The paper is then swallowed or chewed to release the drug. LSD was first synthesized in 1938 from a fungus called ergot, which forms on rye and other cereals. In the 1960s, psychologists experimented with LSD as an adjunct to psychotherapy, but its unpredictable and debilitating side effects—such as paranoid psychoses and schizophrenia—made it quickly lose favor in the medical community.

LSD has lost a lot of its cachet as a party drug since the 1960s—perhaps because it's now sold in much smaller doses (20 to 80 milligrams, according to the DEA, which examined various illicit samples of the drug). In the 1960s, a single dose may have consisted of anywhere from 100 to 200 milligrams.

But some unlikely members of the public are using LSD. A 1997 Monitoring the Future survey revealed some disturbing statistics. Of the 50,000-plus students surveyed, 13.6% of high school seniors, 9.5% of sophomores, and 4.7% of eighth graders had used the drug.

-8-
Dating Tina: Sex on Meth

"NO MATTER WHAT I DO, I CAN'T SHAKE THE FEELING OF WANTING TO GET HIGH...AND HAVE NASTY SEX!"

—GENE

HAVING SEX WITH MULTIPLE PARTNERS IS SORT OF A GAY FANTASY. WITH CRYSTAL YOU LIVE THE FANTASY 24/7. SEX IS A BIG PART OF DRUG ADDICTION. MY PATTERN WAS TO GET HIGH, THEN GO TO THE BATHS FOR DAYS, EVEN WEEKS."

—MEL

"A LOT OF METH USERS ARE SEXUALLY COMPULSIVE. I BELIEVE THERE'S A HIGH CORRELATION BETWEEN CRYSTAL USE AND COMPULSIVE SEXUAL BEHAVIOR. I'VE SEEN A LOT OF MEN START OUT BEING SEXUALLY COMPULSIVE, THEN GO ON TO DEVELOP A METH HABIT."

—JONI LAVICK, DIRECTOR OF MENTAL HEALTH SERVICES AT THE LOS ANGELES GAY & LESBIAN CENTER

In a posting on the KCI message board, a man who calls himself "Cabreu" felt more than a "jumpy rush" when he first began "dating Tina" on his 30th birthday. He says the drug made him feel divine. "You see, Tina was sweet. She gave me energy and insight that seemed to be a God-like feeling of always being aware," Cabreu writes. These days, whenever Cabreu parties, he makes sure "Tina" is invited. Crystal seems to make everything work for Cabreu, who adds, "Have a problem with everyday life? Date Tina. Want to change a flat tire? Hey, Tina, where is the jack?"

Despite his infatuation with the drug, Cabreu says he hasn't "dated Tina" in five weeks. "I won't lie and say that I am ready to break up with her," but he wishes he had never begun what has become a love-hate relationship. "Life with Tina fits nowhere," Cabreu says, and he warns others, "Take my word. Don't go out on that first date."

I Just Can't Get Enough

For Tim, the ex–porn star living in the Silver Lake neighborhood of Los Angeles, crystal was a big tease. "Crystal is the most insane drug I've ever used because it gives you so much intense sexual craving and yet never quenches that thirst no matter how much sex you have. That's when I realized I was in this crystal trap and how bad the drug was," Tim says.

Crystal turned Tim into a sex addict. While crashing on crystal, a friend would give him Valium to soften the crash, which had a restorative effect on Tim. After swallowing the Valium, he would take a cab to his favorite bathhouse. Tim was so addicted to sex, he would go to the bathhouse in the middle of the workday, when no one but the plumbers fixing the sauna were there.

"The main reason crystal is so popular is that it intensifies sex," Richard, the actor, says. Or as Narconon's Web page maintains, "The abuser can experience feelings equivalent to 10 orgasms." This is why crystal "has pretty much devastated our [gay] community," says clinical psychologist Tony Zimbardi, who adds that crystal is harder to treat "than any other substance because of the sex connection to crystal. You get a synergistic effect: natural [neuro-]chemicals like dopamine and norepinephrine and the illegal substance, crystal. It's a case of one plus one equals *five*."

Naturally, sexual compulsives are predisposed to crystal abuse, says Neva Chauppette. "Crystal is 'fuel' for preexisting sex addiction. If you're a sex addict, it's your drug of choice."

Based on her experience as director of mental health services at the L.A. Gay & Lesbian Center, Joni Lavick says crystal is the drug most abused by gay men who have a problem with sexual addiction. "A lot of meth users are sexually compulsive. I believe there's a high correlation between crystal use and compulsive sexual behavior. I've seen a lot of men start out being sexually compulsive, then go on to develop a meth habit."

Crystal is so addictive, says Cathy Reback, who works at the Van Ness Recovery House, the rehab facility in Hollywood, "because of the psychosexual payoffs. If you're having great sex on the drug, you're going to keep using it."

Teenagers have discovered the synergistic effect of combining crystal and sex. Vernon Rosario, a psychiatrist and consultant for Gay and Lesbian Adolescent Social Services (GLASS) in West Hollywood, California, sees patients age 13 through 18 at the youth center. Sadly, not only do his patients use crystal, but these sophisticated teens have found that Viagra is a terrific antidote to "crystal dick" (impotence), which worries Rosario because he says combining the two drugs can cause cardiac arrest, arrhythmia (irregular heartbeat), and strokes.

Do You Mind if I Smoke?

Jeffrey uses the Internet like a giant bathhouse or sex club. When the Los Angeles–based journalist gets off work, instead of stopping by a bar for a drink during happy hour, he logs on to America Online, squeezes into a gay men's chat room, and within minutes (sometimes half an hour on a really slow day), he meets an attractive man and invites him over for sex.

"AOL, Gay.com, PlanetOut—they're just like a sex club...only my bedroom floor isn't sticky," Jeffrey says archly. "I knew I had stumbled onto a major phenomenon in the gay community when two guys in a row I met online asked, 'Do you mind if I smoke?' just before we got naked," Jeffrey says.

"As a former smoker myself, I know what it's like to need an infusion of nicotine," he says. So Jeffrey gave his guests permission to light up, but he also made a mental note that there would be no openmouthed kissing afterward.

What happened next shocked Jeffrey. Both of his dates, after getting his permission, ruffled through a duffel bag and pulled out a filthy glass pipe that looked like an anorexic bong, filled it with a white substance, then torched the bowl with a butane lighter.

Jeffrey had been clean and sober for 22 years and prides himself on always having practiced safe sex. Although Jeffrey has written articles about safer sex and knows all the reasons for practicing it, he haltingly confides that he had unprotected sex with his second date. But even more embarrassing for this dedicated 12-stepper, Jeffrey forgot before foreplay began that his guest had inserted crystal in his rectum—a "booty bump."

Jeffrey experienced just a hint of the powerful synergy of combining sex and methamphetamine, and his experience bears out[3] NIDA's claim that "research indicates that methamphetamine and related psychomotor stimulants can increase the libido in users, in contrast to opiates like heroin which actually decrease the libido." An hour into it, Jeffrey found himself shouting repeatedly at his marginally attractive guest, "This is *the* best sex I have ever had in my life!"

After they finished up, Jeffrey's guest asked for a ride home. "I normally would have been happy to give him a lift," Jeffrey says. "I figure if you're willing to have intimate knowledge of someone, the least you can do is give him a ride afterward."

But after agreeing, Jeffrey looked down at his hands, which were shaking so violently he realized there was no way he could drive. His guilt about having had unsafe sex and not being able to give his sex partner a ride home was compounded when the militantly sober Jeffrey realized that after having sex for four hours, he was experiencing a contact high of the strangest kind: The crystal from his date's rectum had apparently entered Jeffrey's body via his condom-less urethra.

Al Fresco Antics

"I've done some crazy things while on crank," writes Frank on the KCI message board. A bisexual father from West Hollywood, California, Frank has been known to cruise outdoors wearing nothing but a G-string while high on crystal. Needless to say, crystal dramatically enhanced Frank's sex drive—and totally eroded any inhibitions he had. And safe sex went out the door whenever he was high. When he wasn't parading up and down urban alleys nearly nude, Frank liked to dress up "very sexy and dance in front of a mirror for hours on end." Although Frank says he has had some "close calls with the law," he has never been arrested for his louche behavior. Crystal also led to absenteeism at work, and Frank found himself avoiding his children, for which he still feels a great deal of shame.

Frank has stopped using crystal and has embarked on a self-improvement regimen that includes resuming his workouts at a gym. Exercise and other distractions, he hopes, will stop him from using again. "I pray this will be the end of my experience with this evil drug," Frank says.

Reality Bites

Mel knows the math of meth use well. "Crystal is a way of life that's very addictive. Having sex with multiple partners is sort of a gay fantasy. With crystal you live the fantasy 24/7. Sex is a big part of drug addiction. My pattern was to get high, then go to the baths for days, even weeks."

Mel once spent eight days with very little sleep trawling for sex at the Melrose Baths in Los Angeles. Now, sober, he has a hard time believing that he used to spend so much time at what he now thinks of as a filthy facility.

Tina: The Other Woman

Chuck, a Los Angeles–area resident, tells the story of how Tina stole away Todd, the love of his life. "When I met him he was witty, insightful, and intelligent. He was also a crystal addict, and since I had just come out from the [small-town] Midwest, I knew nothing of this insidious drug." Unfortunately, Chuck now knows more than he ever wanted to know about crystal, having witnessed firsthand the drug's destruction of his boyfriend.

"Todd would smoke it day and night," Chuck reports, "eventually getting evicted from his apartment and losing his job. He ended up selling his ass to buy more of the drug, and when that wasn't enough, he would sell it to the clients who bought his ass. He resided primarily at a sleazy gay hotel in Hollywood that was infested with tweakers and every STD one could imagine. At the time, though, I thought everything was OK."

In retrospect Chuck acknowledges what many people who have lived through codependent relationships—as well as many addicts—know: Denial is a very powerful device. Chuck admits he was hard-pressed to end the relationship even after Todd became emotionally abusive. "I told myself that my love for him would be stronger than the drug, and I could handle it and help him. By the end of our relationship he was HIV-positive and a completely different person. I finally had enough and told him that it was 'me or the meth.' He chose the meth."

Unfortunately, six months later, Chuck found out that Todd had given him more than a bunch of heartache: He'd given him HIV as well.

A Blessing in Deep Disguise

Violence seems tragically linked with crystal meth abuse. And the violence doesn't only occur during the crash. Neva Chauppette says that users can also become violent while still riding the crest of the meth wave.

Although most rape victims are female, several of the male crystal users interviewed for this book have suffered this same indignity—West Hollywood clinical psychologist Michael Majeski for one. Michael was walking to a gay bar while high on crystal when he was accosted by a man who appeared to be tweaking too. At first the man innocently asked to bum a cigarette, but then he drew a knife and forced Michael to come with him. Michael was taken to an unoccupied crack house, where he was raped and held hostage for almost 24 hours. During the rape, the man held the knife to Michael's throat. "He threatened to kill me if I didn't submit," Michael recalls. More than 14 years after the sexual assault, he still suffers from post-traumatic stress disorder.

Still, Michael believes the rape was a blessing because it caused him to finally hit bottom and seek help for his numerous addictions, which included alcohol, Valium, Quaaludes, crack, and "black beauties" (an amphetamine)— "anything that was available."

Broken Arrow

Television actor Richard tells a sad story of a dysfunctional relationship he had with a male prostitute, while both were in the throes of crystal. Though they were both abusive, Richard still believes he was the violent one. "It was a physically abusive relationship when we were both crashing. Crystal affects your blood sugar levels and makes you mean," Richard says. Indeed, during one argument, Richard shot his boyfriend with an arrow.

When Richard finally decided to end the relationship and throw his boyfriend out of his home, the other man insisted that it was his home too. Richard then smashed a beer bottle over his own head, called the police, and told them his boyfriend had done it. Richard's boyfriend ended up serving two months in jail for assault. Richard visited him in jail, apologized, and resumed the relationship after his boyfriend's release.

Spoiled Vanilla

Crystal use is such an intense experience for Tom, who lives in Los Angeles, that he's terrified of becoming an addict, even though he's only done it four times. He began using two months prior to being interviewed for this book because his parents were visiting and he was "wigging out." His first encounter with crystal was in bed when a date shoved two "booty bumps" of crystal and the sedative GHB up Tom's anus. "I got fucked for six hours and spent the next three days high on crystal from a single dose," he says, speculating that the drug's lasting intensity was due to his novice status. His first time on crystal was also the first time he had ever had unprotected sex.

While still high from his first experience with crystal, Tom picked up a hunky stranger who was having trouble maintaining an erection with a condom; Tom told him to remove it because he wanted "to get seriously fucked."

Crystal began to affect Tom's health and work habits almost immediately. The drug gave him terrifying heart palpitations and a tightness in his chest that felt like he was having a heart attack. Still high after one meth-fueled sexual encounter, Tom went to the cinema multiplex in West Hollywood where he works as a projectionist and found he couldn't take his mind off drugs and sex—even while having to operate nine film projectors simultaneously. "Work was unbearable. I had to run from projector to projector. I couldn't keep my hands off my dick when I was on crystal, and I started playing with my dick." The heart palpitations soon made Tom lose interest in fondling himself, and he had to lie down on the floor of the projection booth. Eventually, he became so weak that he left work early. That was the first time Tom abandoned the projection booth.

Tom fears he's already psychologically, if not physically, addicted to the drug. "Crystal has ruined me for vanilla sex," Tom laments. It used to be "whenever I meet a guy, he fucks me for 10 minutes. Now [since I began using crystal], if I can't get fucked for seven hours, I don't even want to get together. Crystal has spoiled me."

Tom used to be a zealot about safer sex, but crystal destroyed his resolve. "I'm normally the guy who passes out rubbers," he says. "I want to stay [HIV-] negative, but then crystal rears its ugly head." Another reason why Tom finds himself drawn into the vortex of unsafe sex is that he keeps receiving ultimatums from potential dates who just say no to wearing condoms. He attributes the anti-condom attitude to "gay fatigue: After 10 years of putting on rubbers, we're tired of them," although he claims to engage in unsafe sex only when he uses crystal. Disturbingly, Tom makes the prediction that West Hollywood could become a gay ghost town in 20 years because of the double whammy of crystal and the unpro-tected sex it promotes.

To supplement the minimum wage he earns as a pro-jectionist, Tom has installed a Webcam on his personal computer. Subscribers to Tom's Webcam can pay a fee to watch him have solo sex live in his apartment. Crystal has even impacted this part-time "job" negatively. "When I do my Webcam and jack off, crystal makes my heart beat faster, and that scares me."

Crystal has also lowered Tom's standards for sexual hookups. During one drug run he found himself at the Hollywood Spa, a sex club. "I was so horny I would have let a 70-year-old guy fuck me," he confesses.

Despite the palpitations, chest pains, and problems at work, Tom remains ambivalent about his future with the drug. "Sex will never be the same again without crystal. I don't know if crystal will ever let me go. Tweaker boys have ruined it for the rest of us. They've stolen the normal joy of sex without drugs," Tom says. On the other hand, he says he had terrific sex a few days before the interview, and he wasn't high and his date wore a condom.

Tom has come up with a precarious plan to avoid both crystal and unsafe sex: "I'm going to jack off before I'm offered crystal so I won't crave it for sex," he says.

Spooky Sex

Psychiatry professor Thomas Newton says chronic crystal users "can't perform or get interested in sex unless they're on meth because they've associated crystal with sex for so long." Newton mentions one of his patients, for whom it took eight years to return to normal and enjoy life and sex without the aid of drugs.

Spook, a visitor at Yahoo's MethRecovery site, describes himself as a sex addict and a drug addict—and a very precocious one: He has been having sex under the influence of crystal since the age of 12. At the ripe young age of 22, Spook writes in a message posting that when it comes to his addictions, "I'm really trying hard to break out."

Spook's prescription for dealing with the dual demons of sex and crystal addiction is to "self-isolate" from crystal, which for him "is the door to sex." But his darker side keeps reviving both obsessions and continues to be "a really hard opponent to be up against." After binging on sex and drugs, Spook feels, well, spooked. "Once I commit these acts, I go into a mode of self-hate and swear I'll never do it again." So far he has been unable to keep his promises to stop using. "Sometimes I think I am going mad," he laments.

"Denial Is a Great Thing!"

Forty-seven-year-old Terry is a federal employee in Trenton, New Jersey. Although he doesn't consider himself a sex addict, he loves crystal's ability to turbocharge sex.

When asked if sex was better on crystal, he exclaimed, "Fuck, yeah!" When asked on a scale of one to 10 to rate sex on crystal, Terry says, "Before I began using crystal, sex with my boyfriend was a 15. On crystal, sex is a 25! I mean, he is a seriously good lay, the kind of top most bottoms dream about, and on crystal, the sex is just out of this world." The first time the couple had sex on crystal, Terry says, "it was a religious experience. I kid you not."

Terry's autobiographical profile on AOL says he's "partnered" and only online to chat and to make new friends. But that's not quite accurate: Terry has both a chronically ill lover *and* a boyfriend. "I have a partner who is sick, along with a boyfriend on the side who helps me maintain my sanity," he says.

Terry says he isn't worried about becoming addicted to crystal, because he has so many responsibilities, mainly revolving around his lover, who suffers from the auto-immune disease lupus and recently underwent hip replacement surgery. Terry originally said he's so busy he only uses crystal once a week. Midway through his interview for this book, Terry revised that to twice a week. But he's still not worried about becoming dependent on the drug.

"I have a lot on my plate right now. Perhaps if I lived by myself, or maybe if I didn't have some of the responsibilities I have, I might be more in a position to indulge," Terry says. "I know if things in my life were different, I could definitely become addicted." Since his lover has been in and out of the hospital since surgery, Terry likens his burdensome caregiver role to nursing someone with AIDS. "It's a real mind-fuck," he says.

So far, Terry hasn't engaged in marathon crystal use and sex—the kind that goes on for days without sleeping or eating. His sexual sessions on the drug last only two hours, then he takes the anti-anxiety drug Xanax to get off the crystal roller coaster when coming down from a high.

Terry's boyfriend comes over during his lunch breaks when his lover is well enough to work, and they have through-the-roof sex that Terry says lasts about two hours. During his interview, however, Terry contradicted himself and admitted that while on crystal sex with his boyfriend usually lasts three hours. "On crystal, six hours easy!"

Terry says his ailing lover not only knows about the boyfriend and the lunchtime encounters but also doesn't object. "We all pretend that I'm not having sex with someone else," he says. "Denial is a great thing!" Terry still has sex with his lover, "but it ain't hot." Their enjoyment is hindered by his lover's colostomy bag, which usually gets in the way of lovemaking.

Another reason Terry enjoys sex with his boyfriend so much is that they're both HIV-positive and therefore don't feel the need to use condoms. Terry's lover is HIV-negative, though, so their understandably safer sex can be nerve-racking.

Terry seroconverted in February 2003, and he worries about the damage crystal may do to his immune system, but so far, his "numbers [CD4 T cell count and viral load] are good. As long as they stay good," Terry says he will keep using crystal. He was surprised when told that crystal gobbles up the CD4 T cells that protect against disease.

Bottoms Up

The high from crystal is so pleasurable that it makes some users indifferent to the irony that the drug often interferes with sexual performance.

"People are all bottoming on crystal because they can't get an erection. A friend said that you can't find a top in L.A. because everyone has turned into bottoms," Richard says.

Joseph, a 32-year-old pediatric nurse in Des Moines, Iowa, concedes that crystal made him impotent on the two occasions when he tried it. "But you don't care," he insists. "You don't care that you don't come either." For Joseph, sex on crystal can be intoxicating. "You just can't get enough. It all feels so intense and so good—having your ass played with, getting fucked with dildos, or whatever. It's like you could drive a Mack truck up your ass and it would feel good."

Joseph's crystal-heightened sexcapades are not atypical of users. "Crystal meth seems to 'adhere' to the libido, and it allows sexual gratification to last for hours," notes West Hollywood drug and youth counselor Orlando Rivera. "It's both a stimulant and an anesthetic. You can have [anal] sex for days and not feel any pain."

Sexual Superhero

Henry, a writer-editor on disability leave because of AIDS-related illness, loves using crystal because, "I can have sex for hours and hours on end, sometimes even days. I set a record with a friend last summer: nearly four days of sex, with only brief intervals of rest and food and no sleep at all.

"I become—at least in my head—a sexual superman. I become free of inhibitions that would prevent me from fully exploring certain sexual practices or fetishes," says the Brooklyn resident, whose AOL profile says he likes to use ropes, clamps, feathers, forks, pipes, flogging, tickling, vibrators—"anything that excites."

You don't need a partner to have an intense sexual experience on crystal, but the anesthetic aspect of the drug can create problems. Some users "whack off for days on end, and their penis gets so sore they can't function sexually anymore," Orlando Rivera says.

During the honeymoon period on the drug, crystal not only enhances the libido, it also enhances self-esteem and provides a distorted self-perception. "The misconception among users is that they look great, when in fact they're wasting away," Rivera says.

Rivera speaks from personal experience about the drug's ability to boost one's ego. Before he got clean and sober, he says, "I would go two or three days without sleeping and think I looked gorgeous."

Too Much Fun-raising

Sometimes, it seems almost impossible to separate sex from crystal use. California masseur Paul used to live in a friend's mansion in Laguna Beach. When Paul seroconverted, his roommate threw a charity fund-raiser for the clinic that was treating Paul's HIV. Yet the event became the irony to end all ironies: "The fund-raiser ended up being a drug-infested orgy with lots of unsafe sex going on," Paul recalls.

In order to get sober and avoid temptation, Paul had to move out and away from all the drugs. The owner of the mansion continues to "smoke it constantly, and his brain functions are a mess. He can't remember anything."

Paul's departure from the mansion was the first of two times the drug forced him to change his residence. Recently, a roommate and fellow masseur who was crashing on crystal threw a tantrum because Paul had neglected to change the sheets on the massage table they shared. In what can only be called an overreaction, the roommate threatened to break Paul's neck "like a twig." Paul soon moved out. He says, "I didn't feel comfortable living with him because of his slips"—not to mention death threats.

Sandy Bottom

After spending 10 years in denial about the mayhem his use of methamphetamine had caused, Hector, 42, found himself living in Hollywood at the Coral Sands, which calls itself a motel but is really more like a sex club. Although his memory is foggy on details, Hector does recall buying a large amount of meth, then checking into the Coral Sands. The next thing he remembers is waking up tied to the bed.

Hector's first encounter with the drug occurred 15 years ago, after his father died and his mother moved to another city. He was, in his words, "squatting" in his parents' former home, which had been sold. He decided to drown his sorrows in sex and checked into the Coral Sands, where an obliging stranger injected him with crystal for the first time. It was at the Coral Sands that the connection between crystal and sex became inextricably linked in Hector's mind and body.

"I wish I could shut down the Coral Sands," says substance abuse specialist Orlando Rivera. "I'm not against anonymous sex, but add crystal to the equation and you're leaving yourself open to sexually transmitted diseases because someone high on crystal will not be aware of making the right sexual choices."

The rope Hector was bound with was so tight it made his ankles and wrists bleed. Hector is Latino, and his sex partner at the Coral Sands turned out to be a white supremacist. The man was urinating on Hector when he regained consciousness.

"Urine on an open wound isn't fun, even if you're tweaked," Hector says. "My wrists and ankles were burned raw and bleeding, and [the white supremacist] was obviously getting off on seeing how much pain I was in."

After his dangerous encounter with the racist at the Coral Sands, Hector hit bottom, and he decided to check out Crystal Meth Anonymous. But CMA made Hector's addiction worse. "CMA meetings did not help. I found that when members of the group shared their experiences with crystal, the sex talk was 'triggerish'"—i.e., it made him want to get high again and have sex.

AA Saves the Day

After a brief period of white-knuckle sobriety, Hector hit bottom again. Although he realized he was addicted to sex and drugs, he was still in denial about his concurrent abuse of alcohol. After one last fruitless CMA meeting, he stopped off at a bar for a drink instead of returning home as he had planned. After a series of drinks Hector blacked out for 24 hours, and when he regained consciousness he was too strung out to report to work.

Hector is a high-level executive at an insurance company in Los Angeles, and one of his duties is signing payroll checks. When he didn't show up for work on payday, disgruntled employees phoned him repeatedly. But Hector was too paranoid to answer the phone. "I hadn't even transferred the money into the payroll account," he confesses.

Hector's paranoia is typical of crystal users, according to psychologist Michael Majeski. Paranoia induced by crystal use "can last for a couple of days to a couple of years, even when there was no prior history of paranoia until the individual started using crystal," he says. The clinical term for this phenomenon, according to Neva Chauppette, is "methamphetamine-induced paranoia."

Hector's boss, who has been a mentor figure during the 18 years he's worked at the insurance company, had to be yanked off a plane so that she could return to the office to sign the payroll checks. Hector was too embarrassed to tell her that he was injecting crystal. To save his job—"and my ass"—he told his employer that he was an alcoholic and was going to start attending Alcoholics Anonymous meetings.

"My boss has parented me in so many ways I can't begin to tell you," Hector says. "When I first started working there, she felt I was a diamond in the rough and saw the potential in me. So when she heard that I was going to AA meetings, she was overjoyed."

Hector freely admits he started going to AA under duress: "I wish I could say I had a moment of clarity, but I went to AA out of fear to save my job." But he soon found that listening to the nonsexual accounts of how different group members had hit bottom did not trigger his sexual compulsiveness in the way the talk at CMA meetings had. "I'm grateful to crystal," he says, "because it would have taken me 20 years to get to a meeting if my problem had been alcohol alone."

Simply talking about his drug use during an interview for this book made Hector uncomfortable—not because of the seamy nature of his experiences with the drug but because the conversation made him want to use again, even though in the past three years he'd managed to accumulate nine months of continuous sobriety. After the interview was over, Hector said he planned to pray to stave off another binge of drugs and sex.

"Sex Was My First Love"

When Hector describes his crystal-driven sex drive, it sounds as though he's talking about a lost paramour: "Sex was my first love, and crystal allowed me to have sex for days at a time." His longest binge lasted a marathon 12 days, during which time he didn't sleep. "On other drugs, the high only lasts for an hour at most, and then it's over with. But on crystal you can suppress the climax for days at a time."

Hector didn't even mind the occurrence of "crystal dick"—because on crystal, he felt as though his entire body were having an orgasm, and, as he says, "the euphoria can last for hours, even days."

Crystal desensitized Hector to emotional as well as physical pain. Hector says the drug made him forget "what a piece of shit I was," and more dangerously, made him oblivious to physical discomfort.

Hector says he had "marathon sex" on crystal. Memories of the bad old days were so vivid they caused Hector to switch to the present tense as he described past encounters with the drug. "During marathon sex, I'm bleeding, my genitals have open sores from [using] sex toys, cock rings, ropes. And it's not just 'come fuck me' sex; it's sex driven by bottom-of-the-barrel self-esteem."

Hector always played the masochist role during sex, which included beatings, bondage, torture, and water sports (urine). "I needed the drug to act out the way I felt about myself. I felt I wasn't worthy of anything but being hurt."

A typical night on the town for Hector began at his drug dealer's home, where the full-service dealer obligingly injected him with the drug. Hector's supplier lived near a club called the Meat Rack. "After he shot me up, I'd walk across the street to the bar and get tied up on the patio and then get pissed on by 60 to 70 guys. This went on [until]...the bar closed and they threw me out. Sometimes there would be 10 guys pissing on me at the same time."

Despite his horrific experiences, Hector considers himself relatively lucky. Drug use never got him fired or destroyed his relationship with his current partner of three years. He's held the same job for the past 18 years and works at another job part-time to pay for a house he plans to buy with his lover.

Luckily, Hector says, "Having sex with my lover doesn't make me want to do crystal, because it's a completely different kind of sex. It's not about raging hard-ons or muscle sex. In fact, my lover doesn't even fit the physical mold of what I like...

"But he's the first man I ever had sex with who knows my last name."

Although he's been sober nine months, Hector sounds as though he's describing a lost lover when he recalls the powerful connection between crystal and sex. Hector jokes that his "drug of choice" was sex when he reemphasizes, "Sex was my first love, and crystal allowed me to have sex for days at a time. Sex when you're drunk or high on other drugs lasts at most an hour, and then it's over with. But with crystal you can suppress the climax for days at a time. Then you can have a continual 'orgasm' for days without actually coming."

Maybe his dysphoria was caused by the crash, but Hector remembers feeling depressed when he finally did orgasm. "The climax is almost painful, emotionally and physically, because the climax means sex is over."

Those who manage to become drug-free go through a

✓ "mourning process," according to Neva Chauppette. Most of her clients with crystal abuse problems come to realize that they're never going to have sex as hot or as intense as sex on meth. "So they're not only mourning the loss of the drug but also hot sex," Chauppette says. "A lot of drug counselors try to tell them that regular sex will be just as hot, but I think that's lying, and clients also know it's B.S."

-9-
Crystal—
The Gateway to STDs

"Two-thirds of individuals who tested HIV-positive since June 2003 acknowledged crystal use as a factor in their infection."

—New York City's Callen-Lorde Community Health Center

"Crystal is the superhighway to HIV acquisition and other sexually transmitted diseases."

—Neva Chauppette, clinical psychologist

"No one who does Tina gives a shit about wearing condoms. If they say they do, they're lying."

—George

"I had no self-esteem. I went to sex clubs, bathhouses, had sex with people I normally wouldn't have. I engaged in extreme S/M-oriented sex, lots of anonymous and unprotected sex. Now I have to deal with my sexual acting out, all the people I hurt and lied to."

—Ron

HUGE SALE! BUY CRYSTAL, GET HIV FREE! So read a striking ad depicting a shirtless man with a disco ball for a head. The ad ran on Verizon phone booths in the Chelsea neighborhood of New York City during the month of January 2004 and also received coverage in *The New York Times, Gay City News, HX,* and elsewhere. This innovative campaign was the brainchild of Peter R. Staley, founder of AIDSmeds.com, and Vincent Gagliostro, one of ACT UP's renowned graphic artists.

Staley used $6,000 of his own money to produce the controversial campaign. "These ads are my personal scream about what this drug is doing to my community," he told *HX.* A founding member of both ACT UP and TAG (Treatment Action Group), Staley has chained himself inside government buildings and in 1991 coordinated the inflation of a giant condom over former North Carolina

Senator Jesse Helms's house in Arlington, Virginia.

At the Web site for Being Alive L.A., Staley explains what is probably his most personal act of activism: "I'm a recovering crystal meth addict and long-term AIDS activist in New York City. I'm saddened and angry about what meth is doing to my community. Meth is playing a significant role in the rise of HIV and syphilis infections among gay men in many cities around the U.S.... Meth is destroying many wonderful people all around me when they become addicted."

Staley goes on to say, "There is very little discussion or press about this in New York, and neither the health department or AIDS service organizations are doing or saying much about it. It's a whispered-about epidemic. The ads are my personal response to all of this. They are not meant to be educational. They are a political act. They are meant to provoke discussion and ultimately action by others." Staley continues to encourage people to distribute the ad, which is available at www.AIDSmeds.com/Crystal.htm.

Howard Grossman, one of New York City's best-known AIDS specialists, shares Staley's outrage about the lack of action in response to crystal's scourge. said, "This drug is destroying our community," Grossman told *The New York Times* in January 2004. "It just seems to be getting worse and worse, and no one is doing anything about it." More than half the HIV-positive male patients whom Grossman treats in his private practice blame their seroconversion on methamphetamine use.

Clinical psychologist Michael Majeski says that in the gay community crystal use is "the biggest problem we have now, worse than AIDS." He also estimates that crystal is involved in at least 80% of cases of seroconversion. Majeski's colleague Tony Zimbardi concurs, calling crystal "probably the [number 1] cause of HIV transmission. We're not finding high rates of new infection among gay men who aren't crystal users."

The Official Patient's Sourcebook on Methamphetamine Dependence reports that intravenous drug use causes almost one third of the new cases of HIV infection in the United State; this places crystal IV-users at greater risk than those who snort or smoke the drug. But you don't have to inject crystal to be at heightened risk for AIDS, chlamydia, syphilis, gonorrhea, genital warts, and hepatitis A, B, and C. Crystal use is sometimes accompanied by rough sexual practices that can cause bleeding and skin abrasions. Tears in the tissue paper–thin rectal lining open up vectors or "backdoors" for STD infection.

Many crystal addicts become dehydrated during binges because they're too disoriented or preoccupied to drink liquids. Dehydration also dries out the anus's mucous membrane; a condition that together with the friction from anal penetration "can cause abrasions, tearing, and bleeding," according to Neva Chauppette, who sums up crystal's damaging physical effects as putting the "immune system on overdrive. The body is running full-throttle. You're not resting, eating, or drinking, and you open yourself to all kinds of diseases."

Because sex is so intoxicating on crystal, the drug tends to lengthen sexual encounters, which also increases the risk of STD transmission, although with the abrasions and bleeding. "I'd have sex for 12 hours, just rub myself raw as a top and bottom," says Tyler, a recovering crystal addict who works in health care management, about his marathon sex sessions.

Los Angeles photographer Ron also blames crystal for infecting him with HIV. Before he began using the drug,

Ron was a condom Nazi—a "no glove, no love" kind of guy who used to pass out condoms at circuit parties and bath-houses. "If I had not been doing crystal, I would not be positive. On crystal, I just didn't care [about safe sex]." But Ron isn't depressed about seroconverting. In fact, he embraces his HIV status. "HIV helped me. It never scared me. HIV almost seemed like a fraternity I wanted to become a member of," Ron says. Crystal made him feel like an outsider, but HIV gave him a sense of belonging. "I was willing to hurt myself to join the fraternity" of HIV-positive gay men, he says.

Charles, a 42-year-old Pasadena, California, resident who describes himself as a "stay-at-home dad," didn't practice safe sex while high on crystal. Before he got sober he had contracted syphilis and gonorrhea. Likewise, Redondo Beach, California, accountant Nathan believes he contracted syphilis during unprotected sex when he was tweaking. And David Bouchard—a recovering addict who's now the administrator of the Chabad Residential Treatment Center in Los Angeles—says he thinks that his hepatitis C came from using someone's dirty needle to inject meth. Gary, a computer consultant,contracted syphilis and seroconverted during the 10 years he used crystal before an arrest for dealing the drug made him hit bottom and seek help for his addiction.

A Disease for All Ages

Edwin Bayrd, director of the UCLA AIDS Institute, says the evidence that crystal use promotes seroconversion is at the present time "anecdotal," but he adds that physicians are beginning to see two patterns of seroconversion. "Very young kids, the ones who think they're immortal, are seroconverting, but even more disturbing is the seroconversion among people in their 30s, 40s, and 50s—people who managed to have safe sex for two decades and avoid infection, and now suddenly they're seroconverting. Almost without exception, these patients attribute their seroconversion to drugs, especially crystal."

Death Wish

It's amazing that Chicago silk-screen artist Jeff was lucky enough to use dirty needles and walk away with only Hepatitis C. Jeff's roommate used to keep syringes in a large jar; one day Jeff took one to inject himself with crystal. When the roommate noticed that a syringe was missing, he told Jeff that he had better not have used it. The roommate had recently used it to inject Interferon to treat his Kaposi's sarcoma—cancerous, purplish lesions on the skin.

Sadly, that wasn't the only time Jeff used contaminated needles. "Sometimes I didn't have bleach, and when I used my HIV-positive friends' needles, I just used water to clean them." In retrospect, Jeff considers his use of contaminated needles a suicide attempt. "I used to think, *I hope I get AIDS and die*," he says, remembering the time when he was shooting crystal.

No Cure for Stupidity

"The rising infection rate of AIDS and syphilis is due to meth," says UCLA's Thomas Newton. "People get addicted to it and do all sorts of stupid things because of meth. They end up having so many bad things to face, they need to stay on crystal" to anesthetize themselves against the drug's additional havoc.

Kathy Watt, executive director of the Van Ness Recovery House in Los Angeles, agrees, despite the irony that many users take the drug to escape the reality and ugliness of dealing with HIV and AIDS. Like her colleague Newton, Watt also cites the emotionally anesthetizing or numbing effect of crystal in a difficult world filled with terminal illness and the fear of contracting it. "There are men who want to go on a weekend 'vacation' on meth to just not feel like somebody living with HIV, someone who has to take medications and feels tired all the time."

According to Watt, addicts believe that crystal is "a drug that will numb my mind enough and let me pretend it's the 1970s, and I can have that kind of free sex again—before AIDS, when you could go to a bathhouse and have a good time." Watt hastens to add, "OK, you might have gotten STDs in the '70s, but they weren't fatal like they are now."

Crystal not only beats up users emotionally, it weakens immune systems already under siege from HIV and AIDS. The drug also keeps people from adhering to their drug regimens. As Michael Shernoff, a New York City psychotherapist who treats many HIV-positive crystal addicts, told *Poz* magazine, "Almost every positive man I have worked with has told me that he invariably forgets to take one or more doses of his HIV medication while partying on crystal. So the possibility of spreading a treatment-resistant strain of HIV increases with men who use the drug." Indeed, a 2004 study by Project PILLS (Protease Inhibitor Longitudinal Life Study) showed that patients on HAART who did not use club drugs missed two and a half doses every 60 days, while meth users missed 12 doses. As a result, it's estimated that up to 20% of these new infections involve a virus resistant to some or all of the available treatments.

"The immune system really takes a hit, because crystal use and sex become consuming, preoccupying," says Chauppette. Users often stop eating and sleeping, which further weakens the immune system. "Crystal gobbles up CD4 T cells, and viral load replication triples under the influence of methamphetamine," the doctor explains. "I work exclusively with HIV patients, and 60% to 70% of my patients are [crystal] addicts by the time they get to me."

"Some of my patients become instant bottoms on crystal," Chauppette adds—and she believes bottoms are more likely to contract HIV than tops. But based on his own experience, Tyler disagrees. "People think tops are at lower risk, but I caught [HIV] as a top. I even know who infected me when I was a top. A year later, he died. I saw him in the E.R. at Cedars [Cedars-Sinai Medical Center in Los Angeles]." Tyler says that the guy who infected him "used crystal nonstop. It destroyed his immune system…. Crystal would shred the immune system of a normal [HIV-negative] person, much less someone who has HIV."

The recent AIDS education campaign with the slogan "HIV stops with me" particularly irritates Tyler. "'HIV stops with me'—fuck that! They should say, 'Crystal stops with me.' Then the unsafe sex would stop. How do you educate people about safe sex when they're high on crystal? They don't care about health, just sex."

Tyler wasn't always such a zealot about unprotected sex. He remembers a lost weekend at the San Vicente Inn, a small West Hollywood hotel popular with gay men. Before he got clean and sober, Tyler and a group of his HIV-positive friends were having an orgy in one of the rooms. "It was an awful weekend," he says, recalling that in the middle of an orgy "a 20-something guy stuck his head in the door and asked where all the rubbers were. We said, 'Are you crazy or from Mars? Nobody has safe sex when they're high on crystal.'"

Tyler admits to having starred in a bare-backing video, which led to some embarrassing and amusing complications. Two years ago at Gay Pride in Palm Springs, he was asked to appear as a safer-sex spokesperson and pass out condoms at the parade and festival, but he had to decline: He thought that might be too hypocritical.

Tyler has witnessed firsthand the deadly wake left by AIDS and crystal use. "Crystal is killing friends of mine left and right," he says. "They're dropping like flies right now," and as for 12-step programs, "very few are participating." Tyler's friend, porn star David Glickman, told him shortly before dying in January 2002, "It wasn't HIV that killed me. It was crystal." Crystal use, Tyler insists, "is the gateway to *death*, not just STDs."

Crystal - Self Esteem = HIV

Los Angeles native Anthony believes that crystal was only one of the reasons he seroconverted in 1989. "Part of [contracting AIDS] was due to my drug use, but it's also because I didn't have enough self-esteem to take care of myself," Anthony says. One of the annoying side effects of Anthony's crystal use was that it often caused a breakout of herpes, which he contracted before he started doing crystal.

WebMD has a checklist of tips on how to avoid STDS. (http://my.webmd.com/content/Article/10/2953_511.htm). Crystal users would do well to pay them heed:

❑ Consider that not having sex is the only sure way to prevent STDs.

❏ Use a latex condom every time you have sex. (If you use a lubricant, make sure it's water-based. Oil-based lubricants shred condoms.)

❏ Limit your number of sexual partners. The more partners you have, the more likely you are to contract an STD.

❏ Practice monogamy. This means having sex with only one person. That person must also have sex with only you to reduce your risk.

❏ Choose your sex partners with care. Don't have sex with someone whom you suspect may have an STD.

❏ Get checked for STDs. Don't risk giving the infection to someone else.

❏ Know the signs and symptoms of STDs. Look for them in yourself and your sex partners.

❏ Learn about STDs. The more you know about STDs, the better you can protect yourself.

Information on some common sexually transmitted diseases—chlamydia, syphilis, gonorrhea, hepatitis A through C, and genital warts—can be found in the Resource section of this book, starting on page 237.

−10−
Self-Methicating

"WE'RE ALL CHASING HIGHS. THE HIGH OF
METH AND THE HIGH OF SEX, TO KEEP THE
REALLY DEPRESSING STATE OF AFFAIRS OUT
OF OUR HEADS FOR AS LONG AS POSSIBLE."
— MICHAEL

"WHEN THE BRAIN IS DEPRIVED OF ITS
'MEDICINE,' IT USES ALL OF ITS RESOURCES
TO CONTINUE WITH SELF-MEDICATION."
— JAY, WEBMASTER OF QUITMETH.COM

"DEPRESSION HAS ALWAYS BEEN A PROBLEM
FOR ME, SO THE HIGH I GOT FROM CRANK
WAS A VERY WELCOMED EFFECT."
— FRANK

"CRYSTAL HELPED ME COPE WITH LONELI-
NESS, MY FAMILY. IT HELPED ME FORGET.
BUT IT'S A TRICKY DRUG BECAUSE IT
ALLOWED ME TO THINK EVERYTHING I WAS
DOING WAS THE RIGHT THING, WHEN IN ALL
HONESTY I WAS SCREWING UP."
— JAKE

"WHEN I WAS TWEAKING, I WAS OUT AND
PROUD. BUT TAKE AWAY MY 'MEDICINE,'
AND I WAS RIDDLED WITH INTERNALIZED
HOMOPHOBIA."
— RICHARD

The National Household Survey on Drug Abuse reported in 1996 that an estimated 13 million Americans were currently using illicit drugs. Narconon has observed that drug use "seems to be a problem that has seeped into every facet of American culture." But a drug problem often begins in response to another problem. Narconon says, "The person usually enters into this dangerous affliction because they attempt to compensate for some personal deficiency or life situation. They're depressed, unhappy, or incapable of dealing with their life situations." This phenomenon is known as self-medication.

The self-medication model isn't just metaphorical. "Monitoring the Future," a 2001 study by the NIDA, discovered just how literally crystal was being taken like medicine: "The typical methamphetamine abuser reported using the drug when he or she first got up in the morning, then using approximately every two to four hours… Most of the descriptions of use more closely resembled taking a medication that using a drug for pleasure."

❧ Although crystal and cocaine both belong to the family of drugs called psychostimulants, it's interesting to note that the NIDA study found that coke users didn't fit this self-medication model. "Cocaine abusers reported patterns that fit a picture of recreational use: They began in the evening and continued until all the cocaine on hand had been used," NIDA reported. The differing effects of crystal and cocaine on the brain may explain the drugs' different patterns of use. Crystal produces large amounts of dopamine in the area of the brain that regulates pleasure, but the dopamine is eventually depleted. Cocaine, in contrast, blocks the removal of dopamine, which accumulates in the brain and causes continuous pleasure as opposed to the highs and lows of crystal use, hence the need on the part of crystal users to replenish their intake every two to four hours as opposed to the cocaine users' continuous ingestion of the drug to stop dopamine from leaving the brain.

Bad Medicine

Ex–porn star Tim self-medicated for physical pain—so effectively that he says he wasn't aware that he was suffering from chronic pain until he stopped using crystal six years ago, when he was diagnosed with an anal fissure. For Tim, crystal represented an escape. "Lots of people feel hopeless because they have HIV. Crystal is a 'place' they go where they feel they belong, like bathhouses, where everyone is positive, but you don't have to talk about it." Tim became HIV-positive 15 years ago and was diagnosed with full-blown AIDS nine years ago.

Actor-waiter Mel also self-medicated with crystal. "It was a way for me to continue being gay without thinking about all the friends I lost. Crystal allowed me to continue being promiscuous, because you just don't care when you're high. You don't think through the consequences of your actions. It's all about that millisecond right now."

Bisexual Frank, the father who used to go cruising in only a G-string, is a classic case of self-medicating with drugs.* "Depression has always been a problem for me, so the high I got from crank was a very welcomed effect," he writes on the KCI message board. But for every high, there's a low, and Frank found withdrawal from crystal more painful than his original depression.

Crystal made Brent forget about his HIV status, even though all of his fellow drug users were also HIV-positive. Indeed, crystal made him forget about everything, including work and friends. "I had a lot of absenteeism at work," he says, but somehow he managed to hold on to his job at a car dealership.

Stay-at-home dad Charles also self-medicated with crystal; it made him forget that his career wasn't happening. "I'm an actor, and my career was not turning out the way I thought it would. I had all these grandiose ideas of where my career should be. I was very unhappy with my stalled career. Crystal helped me forget about that...until I came down and had to deal with the death of my career again." The depression caused by the crash made Charles promise himself he'd never use again, but within a few weeks he would forget the pain of withdrawal and return to crystal.

Jonathan, the bartender in Laguna Beach, California, says he uses "self-medication" as an excuse to do crystal all the time. Because of HIV, he has to take a daily regimen of prescription drugs. Crystal, for a while, makes him forget about his HIV status and the frightening realization that he's going to have to take nausea-inducing AIDS medications for the rest of his life.

Porn star and escort Todd self-medicated with crystal "for everything—any little thing that came up, anything to soften the edge, take the edge off things, off life; things like loneliness, being gay, being HIV-positive, being single, being a graduate of the Academy of Dramatic Arts and 18 years later being the star of [the porn video] *Cum and Get It.*"

A Stumble in the Right Direction

Crystal allowed Jake, a 45-year-old Web designer in Los Angeles, to ignore his swollen testicle, even though every time he stood up he felt excruciating pain. "I was doing so much crystal I was too disoriented" to seek medical help at first, Jake says. When he finally managed to see a doctor, his swollen testicle was misdiagnosed as chlamydia, a sexually transmitted disease that can enlarge testicles.

But after a series of tests, including a biopsy and ultrasound, Jake was diagnosed with testicular cancer and the testicle was removed. Jake can't afford a prosthesis, and having only one testicle "makes me uncomfortable about dating because I don't feel complete per se," Jake says. "I can still get an erection, and no one has ever commented on the fact I only have one testicle…. A lot of it's just my self-consciousness."

Crystal also numbed Jake's emotional pain. "Crystal helped me cope with loneliness, my family, it helped me forget. But it's a tricky drug, because it allowed me to think everything I was doing was the right thing, when in all honesty I was screwing up, lying to friends, family, bill collectors. I also lied to myself that I was OK as long as I had something to smoke or snort and a guy in my bed while we watched porn."

Jake stumbled onto sobriety. In June 2002 he moved from San Francisco to Los Angeles, where he finally hit bottom. "After spending every penny I had on crystal and alcohol, I arrived in L.A. penniless, homeless, lonely—just downright empty," Jake muses. "I was going downward, never up."

A homeless shelter called People Assisting the Homeless (PATH) offered Jake an emergency bed for only one night. Jake says he contacted the shelter to help him find a place so he could continue to drink and use drugs. The next day someone at the shelter mentioned that he had just been kicked out of the Van Ness Recovery House in Hollywood, so Jake wandered over there. "I must have been so disoriented that I didn't hear 'recovery' in Van Ness Recovery House. I just thought it was a shelter for gays. It wasn't until I got there that I realized it was a place for sober alcoholics and drug addicts." It was a happy accident that got Jake clean and sober. Since entering the Van Ness House, Jake has managed to stay off drugs and alcohol for 16 months.

The Wrong Ritalin

Silk-screen artist Jeff self-medicated with crystal "just to feel normal." He had injected crystal for 23 years until he checked into an inpatient residential facility for three months, where he was diagnosed with ADHD and bipolar disorder. Jeff believes he self-medicated with crystal to alleviate the symptoms of these psychological disorders. "I couldn't get things done without it," he says. "Most people on speed start 20 projects and never finish. When I was sober, I couldn't finish anything. If I smoked pot, I could get halfway through [a task], but for the most part I just couldn't function without crystal."

These days, Jeff is medicating his conditions with the prescription drugs Neurontin and Wellbutrin. He's only been on the drugs for 3½ weeks and so far he hasn't experienced an improvement, but, he says, "I'm told it may take eight weeks to have an effect."

Even though the prescription drugs haven't yet alleviated his problems with ADHD and bipolar disorder, Jeff says, "My desire [to use crystal] has gone away, because I was so beaten into the ground." He also realizes that no matter how much crystal he would inject, he couldn't get high anymore. By the time his crystal use peaked, Jeff was doing an eight-ball (four grams) during three-day binges. "I needed to do one gram per injection just to feel normal." He blames his inability to get high on the impurity of the drug he was injecting. Because manufacturers are cutting the drug with inexpensive ingredients, Jeff says, "There's a big difference in the quality of meth today versus 10 years ago." In the early 1990s, he says, crystal was the equivalent of whiskey in terms of potency; today, it's more like wine.

The Anti-Anesthetic

Crystal made treatment center administrator David Bouchard forget the ugly world he inhabited; the drug, he says, "made me not responsible for my actions." It allowed him to dismiss his bad behavior by saying, "Oh, well. I was high." Similarly, crystal gave computer consultant Gary a false sense of security—"a false sense of everything. You lose touch with reality. While you're high, you may think you're coping with your problems when they're actually getting worse."

"Crystal makes you forget everything," says specialist Cary Quashen. "The problem is that with crystal, like all other drugs, it stops working [as an emotional pain reliever] after a while. Then you're in trouble. You can't get high."

↳ CrystalRecovery.com notes how people with low self-esteem are especially susceptible to crystal addiction. Adults who were prescribed Ritalin for their ADHD are also susceptible to crystal use. They're "natural" drug addicts because "the chemical transmission path in their brain has already been 'burned in.'" The decision to begin using drugs could be in response to anything ranging from the loss of a boyfriend to a major life crisis. "This causes the person to seek 'help' in the form of drugs or alcohol," the Narconon Web site explains.

Southern California photographer Ron tried to "numb the pain" after he lost his job and home. Friends helped him stay sober for a year, then he relapsed for nine months. After 15 days in an inpatient rehab facility in Minnesota, Ron now has 100 days of sobriety, and he's flourishing in his current 90-day outpatient program. "I'm feeling good. I'm very pleased with how I'm doing," he says.

Torn Up, Inside

After a while, all the dopamine in the world couldn't help Anthony deal with his demons because crystal made him self-destructive. The 38-year-old Los Angeles native living with AIDS says, "I stopped taking my HIV meds because of crystal. I was in denial [about having AIDS] for six to seven years. I used crystal to put it all on the back burner," says Anthony, who is currently in excellent health, even after battling Hodgkin's lymphoma, thrush (a yeast infection of the throat), and pneumonia.

Anthony's Hodgkin's lymphoma has been in remission for five years, and he has accumulated five years of continuous sobriety. Before going on disability due to AIDS, he trained for three and a half years to become an addiction drug counselor, only to quit after just seven months on the job because it was just too stressful.

At first, crystal was extremely effective for self-medicating, Anthony says. It even cured his agoraphobia. Until he started using crystal, Anthony was so filled with anxiety and fear that he found it difficult to step outside his home. "Crystal absolutely helped me with my depression. It gave me more energy. I was afraid to go out of the house. Crystal allowed me to be more social, but the crash just made the lack of energy worse. I had trouble connecting…the crash and fatigue."

Jake had also suffered from agoraphobia before using crystal. He liked to drink alcohol while he smoked or snorted the drug, and when he ran out of alcohol, he had to use more crystal "to make myself believe I looked good enough to go to the store for alcohol."

Cary Quashen, who recently celebrated 23 years of continuous sobriety, recounts a dealing he had with a drug user who suffered from a powerful case of agoraphobia—as a *result* of his crystal use: "Crystal meth has exploded. It's so much more powerful than any other drug around. It's wrecking people. They become so paranoid they don't even want to leave the house for days at a time. I did an intervention the other day, and all [the drug user's] windows were blacked out because he thought he saw leprechauns in the trees, and the leprechauns, he insisted, were out to get him."

At first, crystal got rid of actor Richard's agoraphobia and helped banish his self-hate of being gay. "I started out using crystal recreationally, as we all do, but at the end, it took a lot of 'medicine' to deal with the shame of being a homosexual," says Richard, who was raised a Southern Baptist and had a terrifying father in the military, all of which exacerbated his self-loathing about being gay. "When I was tweaking, I was out and proud. But take away my 'medicine,' and I was riddled with internalized homophobia."

Ironically, after initially getting rid of Richard's agoraphobia, ever-increasing amounts of crystal ended up aggravating it. "I couldn't go out or even leave my bedroom because of [crystal-fueled] paranoia," Richard says. "I couldn't use the phone because I was too emotionally paralyzed to speak."

Richard was what 12-step programs call a "periodic user." He didn't use crystal all the time, but when he binged on the drug, he planned the time "like a general." Before each binge, Richard would rent two dozen porn videos. "I only used [crystal] alone in my room by myself," he says. The binges "mainly involved me and porno." Still, he would only rent four videos at each store—which means he had to hit six video stores to achieve his stash.

Crystal also turned Richard into a compulsive masturbator. While watching porn videos, Richard says, "I'd masturbate till I was raw, then put baby powder on my dick and resume masturbating."

During runs that lasted up to six days with no sleep, Richard's paranoia became so severe he would cover his windows with blankets that he thumbtacked to the window jamb. "As though anybody would want to peek through my windows and look at my naked body," he jokes. "At 48 years of age, me naked isn't a pretty picture."

During his crystal use, he hallucinated that he heard voices. He kept his dog hunkered down in his bedroom fortress—if the dog didn't bark or perk up his ears, Richard would know that the sounds he heard weren't real. He also urinated in a jar in his bedroom because he was too afraid to leave the room for the bathroom.

Withdrawal also turned Richard into Mr. Clean. As he came down from the drug, his agoraphobia would disappear and he would spend an entire day cleaning his bedroom. "I cleaned like a crazy person," he recalls. "To this day, the smell of potpourri strikes terror in my heart, because I used it so much to clean my 'cave.'"

Richard also feared dying of a heart attack caused by using too much crystal. All it took was a big line to cause shortness of breath and numbness in his left arm, a classic sign of an impending heart attack. "I'd make lines [of the drug] as long as your arm," he says. "I knew I was going to die, all covered in Vaseline, paranoid, watching porn videos in my bedroom." His bizarre idea of how to prevent a heart attack was to use more crystal: "I thought maybe a bump would get my heart going again."

Paranoia spilled over into Richard's successful acting career. Especially terrifying were auditions, where he found a roomful of people staring at him. When he did make it to auditions, he says they "were complete disasters. Crystal made me lose all my social skills. There was nothing social about my crystal use. It wasn't even particularly fun, just an obsession."

After six years of continuous sobriety, Richard now realizes the negative impact crystal had on his career. "Slowly, over the years, crystal chipped away at my ambition. All that mattered was my monthly, then biweekly tweaks—planning them, looking forward to them," he says.

Going off crystal created more problems for Richard, and not just the dysphoria that occurs during withdrawal. "When I came off the drug, I'd eat for weeks," he says—at restaurants that offered lavish buffets. "I must be the only speed freak in the history of the drug who got fat. I looked like a beach ball with arms." The weight loss he experienced during crystal binges made the drug all the more beguiling. "I loved the way I looked thin. But I'd regain all the weight I lost and more when I stopped using," Richard says. "A big part of my addiction involved the weight loss."

Losing More Than Just Pounds

Crystal's weight-loss properties made the drug enticing for stay-at-home dad Charles, who lives in Pasadena, California, with his adopted son, Hank, and his lover, who works outside the home. Charles had experienced weight problems since high school but found that he would lose up to 15 pounds during crystal binges that typically lasted three to four days. "Crystal made me super skinny," he says. His 20th high school reunion reinforced his elation over the weight loss. "I had a grand, exciting time. People didn't recognize me because I was thin. In high school I was heavier. [At the reunion] I loved the attention."

Charles has amassed over three years of continuous sobriety. Fortunately for him, when he quit using crystal he didn't experience rebound weight gain, in which the malnourished user overeats to compensate for what he or she didn't eat while on the drug.

Though Charles's substance use began with consuming alcohol, the hangovers caused him to experience violent nausea and terrible headaches, so he "switched brands" to crystal. Charles was a periodic user, which he believes explains why he never hallucinated during his crystal runs, as some of his friends had. "I never imagined the FBI was after me—or any of the other insanity," he says.

When Charles experimented with drugs such as LSD and Ecstasy, he never thought of himself as an addict. It was crystal, he explains, "that brought me to my knees," when withdrawal caused severe depression. Charles feels grateful his crystal use wasn't fatal. "So many people I used to use with are dead now. I believe crystal killed them."

Charles credits his sponsor with giving him a "foundation" in Alcoholics Anonymous and saving his life. Yet Charles's sponsor wasn't able to save his own life; he died of AIDS two years after Charles got sober. It was a sad twist of fate, especially considering that when Charles relapsed from alcohol to crystal, his sponsor told him, "I may have to hold your mother's hand when *we* bury *you*."

Web designer Will self-medicated with crystal for two reasons: poor body image and terminal shyness. Will had been an overweight child, and the excess poundage followed him into a troubled adult life. His lack of social skills vanished after snorting crystal. "I had a lot of social anxiety," he says. "Crystal erased my social inhibitions and made it a lot easier for me to chat with strangers at bars and parties." The drug also made him "very sexually focused and removed my fears of what I wanted to do," which included having unsafe sex.

Crystal relieved Will's self-loathing in a world dominated by the body beautiful. "There's pressure in the gay community to look buff. On crystal, I liked the way I looked," Will says, even though for a while he remained overweight.

But Will wasn't overweight for long after he began using crystal. He began to lose weight rapidly, which made the drug all the more seductive. "The weight loss made me feel more attractive. When I looked in the mirror, I looked great. Then [crystal] turned on me, and suddenly I was too thin." Since he got sober for the second time five years ago, Will has regained 45 of the pounds he lost on crystal.

Michelle is a nurse who spent 12 years using crystal. She began snorting crystal to lose weight. After going from 170 pounds to 115, Michelle was smitten. In addition to making her thin, crystal gave her the energy to put in a full day's worth of work as a nurse, then come home, clean the place, and still have the energy to do "whatever I wanted to do," as Michelle writes on the KCI message board. "I was getting things accomplished left and right,"

But Michelle's honeymoon with crystal didn't last. "After about a year of snorting meth, the effect started to dissipate," she writes. Most of her friends were injecting crystal, and Michelle, despite a phobia for needles, began shooting up to reclaim the elusive high. Intravenous use caused a second honeymoon with the drug: "I thought I had found my savior, my god."

But eventually, Michelle lost her job, her car, her home, and her friends and family because of crystal. The drug also made her a shell of her former self, she adds—literally and figuratively. On crystal she had no emotions except anger and hate, "mostly for myself but also for anyone who questioned" her drug use. A few friends died while she was still using, and Michelle writes that she "couldn't even work up a tear for them. Meth shut me down completely."

Narcotics Anonymous meetings and several stays in

rehab clinics saved Michelle's life. Now that she's sober, she gets "chills" when she recalls what she did—or failed to do—in her 12 years on crystal She warns friends who are thinking about using crystal, and tells friends who are already using to stop. She recommends a rehabilitation program "because this stuff is impossible to quit alone."

Though her recovery has been difficult, Michelle feels grateful that although she knows she will never be "cured," she doesn't have to use crystal today—as 12-steppers like to say: "One day at a time." As soon as she wakes up every morning, she tells herself that no matter how difficult the day becomes, she will not use drugs. And she wants people having trouble with recovery to know this: "It does get better. Please know that there's life after meth, and it's so good."

Vicious Triangle

Another important factor in the phenomenon of self-methication is how intrinsically crystal, HIV, and mental illness are linked: They're three illnesses that feed off one another. Dallas telemarketer Ted, who used crystal to help him deal with chronic depression, seroconverted during marathon sex sessions that typically lasted three days with no sleep. "I wasn't trying to have unsafe sex," Ted confesses, "but part of me wanted to contract HIV, because at least then I'd have an end date to the struggles I've had with depression."

And then there's the suicidal thinking of Chicago artist Jeff, who used his friends' dirty needles to inject crystal. His words are worth quoting again in this context. "I used to think, *I hope I get AIDS and die.*"

For many men, crystal seems a very effective way to

escape the reality and ugliness of dealing with HIV and AIDS. It's worth quoting the words of Van Ness Recovery House executive director Kathy Watt again: "There are men who want to go on a weekend 'vacation' on meth to just not feel like somebody living with HIV."

But then they crash, and depression rears its ugly head, and the cycle starts again. The vicious triangle comes full circle, so to speak.

Faulty Prescription

MethAbuse.net aptly critiques the temptation of using drugs as a means of consolation or solving life's problems. "Drugs…avert emotional and physical pain, providing the user with a temporary and illusionary escape from life. When people are unable to cope with some aspect of their reality and are introduced to drugs, they feel they have perhaps solved the problem itself."

But the solution is false. Self-medication can easily turn into self-destruction. Personal relationships are often destroyed because of drug use. Work performance suffers and may lead to dismissal. The bank account is emptied to pay for more drugs. Eventually, the addict's sole goal revolves around buying, using, and buying more drugs, regardless of the emotional and financial costs. As the Narconon Web site explains, "Drug use becomes the center of [the user's] focus. Soon enough, the person feels the need to use consistently and will do anything to get high."

Drug use has a debilitating snowball effect. In addition to exacerbating existing problems, increasing drug use creates new problems. And the user feels the need to self-medicate all the more just to cope with it all. Eventually, the original problem—the end of a love affair or the loss of a job, for example—may seem minor compared to the nightmare brought on by ever-spiraling drug use. Like many other drugs, crystal is merely a temporary pain-killer. It only creates even more pain for the user and his or her loved ones.

–11–

When Abuse Turns Into Addiction

"THERE'S NO SUCH THING AS SOCIAL CRYSTAL USE. IT'S A DRUG YOU'RE ADDICTED TO. YOU CAN'T SMOKE CRYSTAL LIKE A GENTLEMAN."
—NATHAN

"CRYSTAL MAKES A PERSON FEEL STRONG AND POWERFUL WITHOUT DOING ANYTHING. IF YOU FEEL LIKE YOU'RE GOD, WHAT'S THE POINT OF GETTING UP IN THE MORNING AND GOING TO WORK?"
—UCLA PSYCHIATRIST DR. THOMAS F. NEWTON

"A CASCADE OF NEUROBIOLOGICAL CHANGES ACCOMPANIES THE TRANSITION FROM VOLUNTARY TO COMPULSIVE DRUG USE, BUT ONE OF THE MOST IMPORTANT IS THIS: COCAINE, HEROIN, NICOTINE, AMPHETAMINES AND OTHER ADDICTIVE DRUGS ALTER THE BRAIN'S PLEASURE CIRCUITS."
—*Newsweek*

The Koch Crime Institute has observed that "no one ever tries meth just once." Indeed, CrystalRecovery.com reports that 42% of first-time users report an intense desire to use again, while 84% of second-time users exhibit a pattern of increasing use.

The difference between drug abuse and drug addiction may seem a matter of semantics, but the National Institute on Drug Abuse believes it's a crucial distinction. Drug abuse begins with a conscious choice to use drugs. After a period of abuse, changes in brain chemistry that shut down the natural production of pleasure-inducing neurotransmitters such as dopamine and serotonin can turn drug abuse into what NIDA defines as a "chronic, relapsing illness," or an addiction. Recovering addict Matthew Baughman writes on MethAbuse.net, "Methamphetamine has numerous effects on the user.

It can quickly turn a person into an addict."

√According to Narconon—which claims a 97% success rate despite their claim that "93% of those in traditional treatment return to abuse methamphetamine"—you can tell you're addicted when drugs have become the center of your universe.

That epiphany occurred to David Bouchard, but only after he got sober four years ago. "All my relationships were about drugs. Either you had what I wanted or I had what you wanted. [When I was high] I'd do things I'd never do, like having sex with strange people because they had what I wanted, or getting into a car with somebody out of his mind who shouldn't be driving, or staying at a house where other residents could become volatile and put my life in danger."

√As abuse turns into addiction, drug users "will do anything to get high," the Narconon Web site points out. Users become "difficult to communicate with, withdrawn, and begins to exhibit the strange behaviorism associated with addiction." Drug use begins to affect the personal relationships, work performance, and bank accounts—"anything of personal value."

According to CrystalRecovery.com, "All addictive drugs have two things in common: They produce an initial pleasurable effect, followed by a rebound unpleasant effect." Positive feelings experienced during the high turn into negative feelings as the drug leaves the body. People, places, and things that caused natural pleasure before are avoided and even resented; people, places, and things that facilitate continued drug use are sought out.

This is especially true for crystal. "Anybody who uses crystal impairs his mental and physical health. It's one of those things that you don't realize is happening until it happens," attests Cary Quashen.

Despite the painful withdrawal symptoms suffered by crystal users, Narconon insists that the drug is only psychologically addictive (although others say there is a small physical pull), which is why Narconon says some people may remain casual users. These casual crystal users are sometimes called "chippers" and resemble that rare fraternity of cigarette smokers who are able to sustain their habit with as little as three cigarettes per day. "There's a huge range in how people respond to drugs," says UCLA psychiatrist Thomas Newton. "We know very little about why some people get hooked and others don't. [Chippers] haven't been studied scientifically. Some people do OK and control their use, even though they use a fair amount of crystal. Others end up using crystal daily and become clearly nonfunctional."

On the Edge

Back in Des Moines, Iowa, Joseph stands on a precipice overlooking possible addiction. He's already lost a few friends to crystal. "They got so tweaked out their whole lives fell apart. They abandoned anything that did not have to do with crystal and sex." Yet Joseph has no plans to abstain permanently. Perhaps because he's never had a painful crash on crystal, Joseph envisions using the drug again, but only with a lover "for some sexual exploration with him," not with a casual date.

As his job as a pediatric nurse suggests, Joseph loves children and plans to adopt a child as a single parent. Would having a child put an end to his crystal use? "I wouldn't use while the child was around, but perhaps when 'Junior' went away to camp…. I would be much more responsible about my crystal use if I had a child."

As for Joseph's assertion that he can handle his occasional use of crystal, Kevin Kurth remains skeptical. Kevin is the mental health and education manager for Being Alive, a peer-based AIDS service organization in West Hollywood, California, that works in tandem with other groups to educate people about the connection between crystal use, unsafe sex, and AIDS. "We get a lot of people who say, 'I use crystal once in a while, and it's not a problem for me,'" Kevin says. "Then the next time we see them, they're 20 pounds lighter, they've lost some teeth, and sometimes they've lost their house, their job." Tooth loss is a problem for tweakers, Kevin notes, because they often go for days without eating while they binge on the drug.

Vernon has only been using crystal for the past year. In a message posted at Yahoo's MethRecovery site, Vernon wrote that he planned to stop using crystal sometime during the coming week after his posting and hoped someone would read what he wrote and offer emotional support. Vernon is shy and finds it difficult to go up to strangers at 12-step meetings and say, "You're going to be my support friend—now!" To achieve sobriety, he plans to use a combination of detox (usually accomplished by giving the user a sedative like Xanax or Ativan to smooth out the bumps in the crash) and psychotherapy.

Vernon is one of those rare drug addicts who has decided to get clean and sober early in his addiction. He hasn't hit bottom yet, but he is prescient enough to realize he's approaching full-blown addiction: "I have not reached a severe stage [of addiction], but I can see myself heading there."

Strike Three: You're Out

Narconon divides crystal users' behavior into three patterns: low-intensity, binge, and high-intensity. Low-intensity abusers, Narconon claims, aren't addicted to crystal and only swallow or snort it. Binge and high-intensity abusers are psychologically addicted and smoke or inject the drug.

Narconon views low-intensity abusers as using crystal in the way other people use nicotine or caffeine. Low-intensity abusers are often overachievers who do crystal to be more productive at work or at home. They also value the drug's weight-loss properties. Low-intensity abusers, according to Narconon, "frequently hold jobs, raise families, and otherwise function normally"; for example, pilots and truck drivers often use it to stay awake on long trips.

Designing Under the Influence

Most of Wesley's friends are addicted to crystal. Twelve have committed suicide after using the drug "for days on end." They killed themselves while experiencing the dysphoria that typically accompanies withdrawal or crashing on the drug.

Wesley uses crystal once or twice a month and only in small amounts. He has no fear of becoming addicted or committing suicide because "I don't have an addictive personality, and I'm not a depressive type—just a happy, preppy Leo. I'm very down to earth. I lead a charmed life. I love my life too much." Wesley is a member of Mensa with an I.Q. of 186, and he believes he is smart enough to avoid his suicidal friends' fate. He also makes sure he's not around when his friends go on crystal binges.

"I won't watch people I love self-destruct," he says.

Both of Wesley's parents are psychiatrists at Bellevue Hospital in New York City, and both know of his drug use. He claims they aren't worried because they know "how down to earth I am."

While most gay men use crystal for marathon sex or dancing in clubs all night, the work ethic fuels Wesley's desire for the drug. The last time he did crystal was a month ago, and even though he says he only took a small amount, he stayed up for 24 hours…working. Wesley is a fashion designer and illustrator. "My designs are very detailed, and crystal improved my focus and concentration," he says. Before moving to Atlanta, Wesley lived in Manhattan, where he says most fashion designers and models use crystal.

John White, a former drug counselor at the L.A. Gay and Lesbian Center, says, "One of the things my patients told me that they really liked about crystal is that it helps them concentrate and focus their mind. Without crystal, they fritter about, can't quite attend to something they would like to. Crystal seems to do two things: calm [users] down and help them focus."

But drug treatment administrator David Bouchard believes the increased productivity that users claim crystal gives them is fleeting: "People say they get a lot accomplished, but that's only at the beginning. Once they become addicted, they don't get shit done. They just go in circles."

Even though Narconon claims low-intensity users aren't psychologically addicted to crystal, they also say that "these individuals are one step away from becoming binge abusers. They already know the stimulating effect that methamphetamine provides them by swallowing or snorting the drug, but they have not experienced the euphoric rush associated with smoking or injecting it." Narconon

warns low-intensity users that all they have to do is switch
to smoking or injecting crystal in order to graduate to the
second pattern of abuse: binging.

The Big Flood

The euphoric rush that accompanies smoking or injecting crystal makes the drug psychologically addictive,
Narconon maintains, because those two methods of ingestion trigger the adrenal gland to release adrenaline and create the "explosive release of dopamine in the pleasure center of the brain." Unlike the naturally occurring neurotransmitters in the brain, the release of which John White com-
pares to "little drips," methamphetamine floods the pleasure center of the brain with tsunamis of neurotransmitters.

Despite being hit with floods of exhilaration, binge users
aren't usually pleasant to be around. Narconon says, "They
often feel aggressively smarter and become argumentative,
often interrupting other people and finishing their sentences."

After the rush wears off, crystal isn't finished with the
abuser, who then experiences a high that can last four to 24
hours. Binging refers to nonstop use of crystal, during
which time the rush becomes less powerful with every puff
or injection as the abuser tries to recapture the original
euphoria by using more of the drug. While binging, "the
abuser becomes hyperactive both mentally and physically,"
Narconon says. Binges without sleep and minimal food can
last three to 15 days.

Speed Freaks

The third and most severe type of crystal abuse involves
high-intensity users. Like binge users, high-intensity users

are forever and fruitlessly pursuing the original rush by ingesting ever larger amounts of the drug. The primary difference between bingers and high-intensity users is that the latter use more crystal, which has earned them the nickname "speed freaks" and makes their existence solely drug-based.

Tweaking comes at the end of the binge, when no matter how much crystal the addict ingests, he or she is unable get high. Tweaking causes severe depression, which is often treated with alcohol or heroin. "A methamphetamine abuser is most dangerous when tweaking... the abuser has probably not slept in three to 15 days and consequently will be extremely irritable." This frustration at not being able to get high can make users unpredictable and dangerous.

Another reason treatment crystal use has such a high failure rate is that on the surface, the tweaking drug user appears so normal that friends and family may not be aware of their loved one's major problem with methamphetamine. There is none of the slurred speech or glassy eyes that come with alcohol and other drugs; unlike the stumbling drunk, a tweaker's movements are coordinated.

Look closer and you'll see the high-intensity tweaker's eyes moving 10 times faster than normal—or possibly his or her compulsive eye-rolling. His voice may have a slight quiver. His movements may be exaggerated, "because he is overstimulated," Narconon says. His thinking may be scattered and "subject to paranoid delusions."

Narconon warns that it's impossible to predict what may prompt a tweaker to become violent: "A tweaker exists in his own world, seeing and hearing things that no one else can perceive. His hallucinations are so vivid that they seem real." If his paranoia is triggered, the tweaker may feel

others—most often, police officers, but also even a friend—
is a threat. Mental impairment can be so severe that
hostage-taking can occur at this stage in the drug cycle.

If the tweaker has added alcohol to the mix to alleviate
the discomfort of tweaking, "he becomes a disinhibited
tweaker." During this stage, it's impossible to reason with
the tweaker, and he may appear merely drunk, albeit a hel-
laciously dangerous drunk.

A number of authoritative sources, among them
Narconon, have linked methamphetamine abuse to incidences of domestic violence and traffic accidents. A
tweaker behind the wheel of a car is a terrifying image. He
may hallucinate that moving shapes are threatening him,
and so he may increase his speed or drive erratically to
escape them. Tweakers also have a tendency to carry con-
cealed weapons, because their paranoia makes them feel
unsafe. They're also often involved in "spur-of-the-
moment crimes such as purse-snatching, strong-arm rob-
beries, assaults with a weapon, burglaries, and thefts of
motor vehicles," Narconon says.

The nightmare of tweaking is followed by the relative
mercy of the crash. The abuser is usually unconscious
or semiconscious during most of the crash and may fit-
fully sleep for one to three days. After the abuser awak-
ens, he returns to a so-called "normal state." Narconon
points out that "normal" is a relative term in this context, since the abuser's mental and physical capabilities
have declined considerably from before he or she first
used crystal. This state lasts from two to 14 days; as the
amount of crystal ingested increases, the period of nor-
mality decreases.

Withdrawal, the last stage of high-intensity crystal use,
at first is a continuation of the normal stage. The user

suffers no ill effects such as depression or physical discomfort during the early withdrawal period. Within 30 to 90 days, however, the addict begins to experience depression and anhedonia, the inability to receive pleasure from previously pleasurable activities.

"When you stop using crystal, you feel like you've been run over by a truck—no energy whatsoever," says actor and long-term HIV survivor Mel. "You're very depressed and prefer to stay in bed for two weeks after a binge."

Lethargy is accompanied by a craving to do more crystal. During the period of craving, the addict often becomes suicidal. However, if the addict resumes meth use, all the craving, lethargy, and suicidal ideation magically disappear, which helps explain why Narconon calls crystal addiction a "chronic, relapsing illness" and cites a treatment success rate of only 7%.

The lingering threat of self-destructive urges also explains one of the ideological mainstays of 12-step programs: Relapse is part of recovery. Realizing this helps sober alcoholics or drug addicts who relapse not to despair: They will be welcomed back when they are ready to try again. "Rarely have I seen one or even two admissions into treatment facilities as sufficient to deal with the drug problem," says psychologist Neva Chauppette. "It usually takes three to four admissions."

Mel believes the disappearance of uncomfortable feelings after a brief period of abstinence is part of what makes the drug so addictive. "After the binge, you feel awful, you promise yourself you'll never use again, but two weeks later you feel good and you resume drug use. That's what's so pernicious about crystal. I promised myself a dozen times I'd never do it again…and I did it again."

Speeding Up

Web designer Will remembers making the transition from occasional to frequent use of crystal. After six years in CMA, Will has five years of continuous sobriety. He relapsed once after one year in the program, and his slip was triggered by a common culprit: sex. "I met someone at a gay bar who was using. I went home with him and ended up using myself."

The progression of Will's disease was similar to that of many other users: His weekend-only use slowly began overlapping into Monday so that he could deal with the hangover from the weekend binge. Then Will began using on Thursdays because it was "almost the weekend, so why not start using on Thursday?"

"I dabbled in recreational use, then it became more frequent and intense," Will says. "It was a clear progression." The amount of the drug he ingested also increased with time, as did the severity of his withdrawal from it: "The crash got worse, especially the depression that came with crashing."

Daily Doses: A Career Killer

Michael, 29, long ago made the transition from drug abuser to drug addict. These days he injects one half of a gram to one gram twice a day, every day. His habit only costs him $100 a week, because his dealer sells him crystal at wholesale prices since he buys so much of the drug. A former teacher, this Boston native sometimes smokes the drug, but says he prefers injecting it, "because the high is better."

Although Michael's crystal use hasn't impacted him too

badly financially, it's been a career killer. He was working on a doctorate in education before he started using crystal. "I was in graduate school, majoring in secondary education," he remembers, "and I decided it was not the best time to be spending all that money on school if I'm going to be fucking up. I kept missing classes and falling behind in my schoolwork."

Crystal has also impacted Michael's health. While high, he has a lot of "unprotected sex." At last check he was HIV-negative, but he keeps putting off his next test. "I'm not expecting good news when I get tested for HIV," he says. "I don't know when I'll take the test again."

Michael's IV crystal use gave rise to another health problem. Although he always cleaned the needles he used with Clorox bleach, his self-injections still caused nasty skin abscesses. "I'm on antibiotics right now because of that," he says.

Abscesses notwithstanding, Michael has never suffered the dysphoria of drug withdrawal. "I'm always high, so I never crash," he quips. Although he has never hit bottom, Michael has tried to quit on his own after he got back together with an ex-beau, who was "very antidrug." The renewed relationship lasted only a month and a half, but Michael insists it wasn't his drug use that sabotaged it.

Without the help of therapy or a 12-step program, Michael's periods of white-knuckle sobriety have never lasted more than a week. He is a fatalist who believes that there's some karma in his inability to quit. During one period of sobriety, he was searching for his library card when a packet of crystal fell out of his wallet, almost immediately ending his sobriety.

Many experts have cited guilt as one of the classic signs of addiction—substance abuse authority Robert V. Seliger made that observation over half a century ago. Yet Michael insists that he never feels guilt about his drug use. He does think about cutting back, though, because he knows "You get too crazy, doing too much, spending too much money. You can't be fucked up all the time."

Another one of Seliger's telltale signs of addiction is that the user rejects friends' criticism of his or her habit. That *has* happened to Michael. "I know they're probably right," he says, then adds defensively, "but it's none of their business. They're not paying my bill "I've seen them get crazy on other drugs. They're worse than I am."

Disorderly Business

Bob, a nurse who posted a despairing message on the KCI message board, blames crystal for the suspension of his nursing license for five years. In fact, the board of nursing in his state threatened to yank his license permanently due to extreme negligence on the job, but Bob voluntarily surrendered it. At the time of the posting, he had three years left before he could attempt to resume his career—if the board ever lets him.

Bob reports that meth use is common in his profession. "You cannot believe all the meth-addicted nurses out there still providing care in our hospitals and nursing homes," Bob asserts. "[Crystal is] a great drug until you start making medication errors because you have been up for three days and can't focus. You hurry through your documentation and charting in order to make up for the time you tweaked out on a dressing change [changing a bandage]. But one mistake simply leads to another, for meth-addicted caregivers. "So you keep on making medication errors," Bob says, "and then you actually kill a patient because you gave them too much of a type of medication or simply forgot to give them the medication altogether. Try explaining *that* to the doctor and family members."

Bob has repeatedly tried quitting, but his sobriety never lasts long. "I'll go for a week [without crystal], then completely wig out," he writes. "My body is so physically addicted that I've convinced myself I can't quit. It sucks."

Bob has sought help for his problem, but nothing seems to stop him from relapsing. He stopped attending Narcotics Anonymous meetings after two of his sponsors relapsed. Bob is an atheist, and he had problems with Narcotics Anonymous' emphasis on using God to fill the "hole" that drugs had previously filled.

But despite his setback with Narcotics Anonymous, Bob goes to intensive outpatient IOP meetings twice a week, but they have so far been unable to help. Friends in Narcotics Anonymous told him that he would know when it was time to quit, but Bob isn't buying this rosy scenario. He's well aware that it was time to quit using a long time ago. "Fuck that! Tell me whatever the fuck you want, but I can't quit," Bob says.

Working to Stay Clean

David is a 50-year-old small-business owner who began doing various forms of speed in 1971. But it wasn't until the early 1990s that he began using crystal on a daily basis, turning his abuse into addiction.

David has been clean and sober for five years now, but his abstinence takes the form of white-knuckle sobriety. By sheer force of will, without professional treatment or participation in a 12-step program, he has not touched the drug. Still, abstinence is a daily struggle, and David is terrified he will resume his drug use: "I *am* an addict. It's very hard for me to stay clean."

His preferred methods of ingesting were snorting and shoving the drug up his rectum. A friend introduced him to the mechanics of this last method, which is not the same as a booty bump. David was told to buy gel caps at a pharmacy, empty them, then stuff a capsule with crystal before inserting it. "When the gel cap dissolves, [crystal] is absorbed by the lining of the colon instantly," David says.

At first, crystal seemed to allow him to focus on work, but the drug also increased his libido so much that he became unable to concentrate on the job. "It got to be that all I wanted was drugs and sex," David says.

Eventually David had to quit crystal, but not because he hit bottom. Rather, family responsibilities, a terminally ill lover, and a powerful work ethic motivated him to get clean. David was taking care of his 85-year-old father—and still does—when his lover was diagnosed with brain cancer in 1998. "If it weren't for my lover, I'd be dead by now," David says. Even though he watched his partner die in 2001, David has managed to avoid a relapse.

David still runs the answering service he and his lover created together. And despite five years of uninterrupted sobriety, David still considers himself a drug addict, saying "I'm not using, but I want to."

The Jonathan Method

Southern California bartender Jonathan should be the poster boy for the understanding of addiction as a "chronic, relapsing illness." Jonathan had accumulated eight days of sobriety when he was interviewed for this book. During his most recent binge prior to the interview, he had ingested an entire gram, the most crystal he's used during one "run," and spent four days on the drug without sleeping. Prior to that binge, Jonathan had managed to achieve 13 days of sobriety.

Overwhelmed with remorse over his repeated binges—they've been averaging twice a month—Jonathan smashed his glass pipe and poured water into the plastic bag the crystal came in to get rid of any drug residue stuck in the corners of the bag. He even sprayed Fantastik on the countertop where he had snorted to remove any residue that might tempt him to use again over the next few days. It takes him approximately four days to recover physically from a run.

Jonathan has been in and out of 12-step meetings, and they seem to help a little in preventing the relapses. "I've realized that the 'Jonathan Method' isn't working," he admits. The usual triggers prompted his most recent drug run: shortness of breath and feelings of powerlessness. After the binge ended, he did what he often does; he called all his dealers and told them never to sell him crystal again. Jonathan has gone so far as to ask his favorite dealer to delete his phone number from his cell phone memory. "He said 'no problem'—but I know where he lives."

Jonathan wishes the drug dealer would get arrested—for his own sake and that of other users. "He's such an endangerment to society. His crystal is all prepackaged and available to anybody who wants to buy it."

But for Jonathan, temptation is omnipresent. After dumping his dealer, Jonathan admits he went to a sex club and bought crystal from another patron: "Sex and drugs: It's like walking past a dealer's open door in the middle of a great sex session."

Tricks and Treats

Certainly, Todd can attest that crystal addiction is a "chronic, relapsing illness." The 38-year-old porn star and escort did crystal for only six months and then was clean for 10 years before he finally relapsed.

In May 2003, Todd's life seemed to be going well. He had become a major adult video star and a sought-after escort and photo model. He was making a fortune. Once, while he was dancing at a club, he was offered crystal and snorted some. Drug experts claim that people who use crystal and cocaine are always chasing the unattainable high of the first time, but Todd's experience on the dance floor suggests that's not always true—perhaps because it had been a decade since he last tweaked.

"It was like doing crystal for the first time all over again," Todd says of catching the dragon the second time. "I absolutely loved it."

Shortly thereafter, Todd flew to New York City to appear in a porn video, and his crystal use increased dramatically on the shoot. "Everyone in New York I bumped into was either an addict or a dealer, it seemed," he says. "I was very out of control."

By August 2003, Todd had gone from snorting to smoking crystal, and he says, "that's when everything completely started unraveling." What had been a "vacation drug" turned into daily usage after he began smoking. Smoking, he says, provides a "softer high" than snorting. He cites August 16, 2003, as the exact date his crystal use became a "chronic, relapsing illness."

It was during a trip to San Francisco where he was to shoot a video that Todd hit what he calls a "high bottom"— a bottom, but not a devastating one. Todd managed to abstain from crystal use during the video shoot and only took the benzodiazepines and liquid opium that were prescribed by his physician for anxiety and irritable bowel syndrome. Todd calls his physician "Dr. Feel Good" because "he will prescribe anything you ask for." The kinky doctor, himself an alcoholic, considers his HIV-positive patients, which include Todd, "dead meat" anyway.

On Todd's last night in San Francisco, a man who'd hired him for sex wanted to use crystal. When the man learned of Todd's past problems with the drug, he asked if Todd wanted to call a friend who was helping him stay clean. That way Todd wouldn't be tempted while the man did crystal. "I said, 'No, it's late, and my friend's already in bed,'" Todd recalls. He ended up smoking crystal all night with his client.

When Todd returned to Los Angeles, he was so dehydrated and underweight that he almost fainted at the airport. Todd managed to stay away from the drug for a week after his return, but then he went online and bumped into a buddy who invited him over to use crystal. "I hit that pipe as soon as I could. I didn't even shower. I just wanted to get crystal," he says. The need to use *now* can be so powerful that lacking a glass pipe, some addicts will use a broken lightbulb to heat up their crystal, Recovery.com reports.

Todd then called another drug buddy, "and I just totally broke down. I had a moment of clarity, and I realized how powerless I was against the drug. My life had become unmanageable."

Todd's life was about to become even more unmanageable. "I begged [the second buddy] to let me come over to his place, because I knew if I went back to the first place, I would use again." His second friend paused for a long time, then with embarrassment revealed that he had been up all night doing crystal and having sex with someone who was still there. Then his friend asked, "Can we come over and fuck you?"

Todd hung up, disgusted, and called another friend for help. But he only received yet another invitation to use crystal, and this time he accepted. "I was dying on the inside. I proceeded to get very loaded," he says. He smoked the drug that night, inhaling deeply and holding the smoke in his mouth and lungs for a long time after each puff, which Todd feels reflected a death wish on his part. "You're not supposed to hold the smoke in because it can kill you, but I wanted to die of a heart attack."

This time crystal didn't have its usual euphoric effect. Todd remembers becoming increasingly agitated and emotional. "It was hard to hold back tears with each hit of the pipe," he says.

When interviewed for this book, Todd had accrued 32 days of continuous sobriety. For someone so newly sober, he seemed to be in amazing mental and physical health, with none of the jitters, lack of focus, or depression that often accompany withdrawal from the drug—especially since he'd also had to go through withdrawal from the benzodiazepines and liquid opium. Once he stopped using crystal, his irritable bowel syndrome went away, and he no longer needed the liquid opium, though he warns that opium withdrawal was the most painful of all.

Clean, sober, and still healthy despite seroconverting over a decade ago, Todd has begun to take a painful look at his livelihood, especially in light of how HIV has devastated the porn industry. "I work now as a full-time escort with a solid clientele base both in L.A. and in New York," he says, adding. "I know very few porn stars who aren't HIV-positive—escorts as well."

Thankfully, Todd is now applying for nonporn jobs. "I'm up for a real job tomorrow in [retail] sales," he says. Since he got sober, he says porn and prostitution are no longer "fun." "Escorting isn't as glamorous as it sounds," he confides. "And I'm 38. How much longer can I turn a trick?"

Crystal fueled Todd's fancy for porn and prostitution. "I never realized how much crystal made me want to do porn and escort. I'm a much more conservative person, who needs a lot more structure and stability than those kinds of professions usually allow," he says. On the other hand, Todd candidly observes that has friends who are clean and sober and still love working as prostitutes and appearing in adult videos.

As for his crystal addiction being a chronic illness, Todd is filled with hope that he can beat that definition of drug addiction. "I have a great sponsor, close friends in the program, and I'm optimistic about staying clean."

-12-

The Hardest Addiction to Treat

"[Meth] may be as addictive as anything you can get your hands on."
—Edwin Bayrd, executive director of the UCLA AIDS Institute

√ "Even if meth users acknowledge the danger of their actions, only 6% of them are able to stay sober—by far, the lowest recovery percentage for any drug."
—Arielle Chavkin, from a study on Tufts University Wire

"I don't have any great treatment options right now. This drug really terrifies me, and I think what we're seeing is the tip of the iceberg."
—Dawn Harbatkin, medical director at New York City's Callen-Lorde Community Health Center

Dawn Harbatkin, medical director of New York City's Callen-Lorde Community Health Center, told *The New York Times* in January 2004, "I don't have any great treatment options right now. This drug really terrifies me, and I think what we're seeing is the tip of the iceberg." Callen-Lorde, the city's largest private clinic for gay men and lesbians, has been conducting a pilot study on ways to treat crystal meth addiction. But Harbatkin is not hopeful. "When it comes to crystal, there is no moderation," she says.

Alex Stalcup, the medical director of the New Leaf Treatment Center in Lafayette, California, has been treating meth addicts for almost half a century and offers this discouraging prognosis. "Meth is the most dangerous drug I have ever seen." Until a treatment or cure for meth addiction is found, Stalcup despairs of crystal users ever achieving permanent remission from their illness. "The hell starts when [meth addicts] get sober and find that meth has stripped out their higher functioning, much of which won't come back."

At present, there are no drugs on the market for treating meth abuse and addiction, according to Bankole A. Johnson, M.D., Ph.D., a professor of psychiatry and pharmacology at the University of Texas Health Science Center. But the need for a "silver bullet" is growing concurrently with the number of people who need help with meth—especially since right now the prospects for addicts who want to get off the drug aren't very encouraging. As noted at the start of this chapter, a March 2003 article by Arielle Chavkin, posted on the Tufts University Wire, reported that only 6% of meth users attempting to stay off the drug were successful.

Social Solutions

So what is to be done about the intractable problem of crystal addiction? According to Vernon Rosario, a clinical instructor in psychiatry at the UCLA Neuropsychiatric Institute who has also worked with Gay and Lesbian Adolescent Social Services in West Hollywood, California, We need more treatment programs, more public awareness in the gay community about the seriousness of the issue and the consequences of crystal use and addiction. People need to know the total function impairment caused by crystal. People can't keep jobs or relationships. They engage in unsafe sex. They need to know about the depression that accompanies the withdrawal from crystal, and how crystal leads to other drug use."

Although crystal addiction is very difficult to treat, Rosario offers addicts hope that they can overcome their illness: "Twelve-step programs like Alcoholics Anonymous are extremely effective for some people. They're as effective as any treatment we have." For those who find the religious elements of 12-step programs problematic— Step Three, for example, says, "We made a decision to turn our will and our lives over to the care of God as we understood Him"—Rosario recommends individual psychotherapy instead.

Los Angeles journalist Jeffrey, a professed connoisseur of 12-step programs, was always struck by the small amount of sober time crystal users had compared to other drug addicts. While alcoholics shared at A.A. meetings that they had accumulated many years of sobriety, he said, participants in Crystal Meth Anonymous meetings measured their sober time in weeks or more often in days.

Hope for Help

Bankole Johnson is also the lead researcher for a study of the drug ondansetron (brand name Zofran) and its effectiveness in treating meth addicts at the Southwest Texas Addiction Research and Technology Center at the University of Texas.

Ondansetron, which is prescribed for the nausea and vomiting that accompany chemotherapy, has shown some promise in reducing the cravings of early onset alcoholics by increasing production of the pleasure-enhancing neurotransmitter serotonin. Some alcoholic patients who participated in a study of ondansetron found that they drank less, while others achieved total abstinence from alcohol.

There's hope that ondansetron may also decrease the cravings of crystal users. "We're very encouraged by this promising compound [ondansetron], since we're trying to find medication where none currently exists," Johnson says. The search for effective treatment, Johnson points out, is especially compelling since methamphetamine, which in the past had been used almost exclusively by men, "now involves a different population, which includes...children."

But the effect of ondansetron will likely disappoint chronic meth users. Whereas the euphoria experienced by drug users comes from increased levels of dopamine in the brain, ondansetron increases levels of serotonin, which reduces dopamine levels, which means crystal users taking ondansetron will no longer enjoy the euphoria caused by an increase in dopamine. The theory behind ondansetron's therapeutic use is that if you take away the high, users will lose interest in crystal.

Drug treatment administrator David Bouchard—who dropped out of high school only to use crystal for 23 years—was one of the lucky ones. It didn't take an experimental drug to make him see the light. Instead, he made a "paradigm shift" and returned to school. "I just made a choice," he says. "This was not how I envisioned my life at 36. My thinking was changed. I was clear that this was not the path I wanted to continue down, and it was up to me to change it. I was an orphan and ran away from a residential institution for boys when I was 16. I moved to Hollywood. That's when the vicious cycle of drugs started."

In *Cocaine Addiction: Theory, Research, and Treatment*, Jerome J. Platt cites two studies done in the 1970s indicating that methamphetamine causes severe depletion of the brain's pleasure-enhancing neurotransmitter norepinephrine. The antidepressant desipramine (brand name Norpramin) blocks depletion of norepinephrine, and Platt hypothesized that giving the antidepressant to drug addicts might relieve their cravings.

Platt prescribed desipramine to 22 addicts—eight were methamphetamine-dependent and 14 were cocaine-dependent. The results after only seven days were promising. Remarkably, 86% of the test subjects said they had stopped using drugs within two to seven days after the study began. Some of the test subjects, however, were less than forthcoming, because only 68% of the subjects' urine samples tested negative for cocaine or meth. Nevertheless, 68% is still an impressive instance of remission in treating the intractable disease of crystal addiction.

Other psychopharmacologists have tried using drugs prescribed for cocaine withdrawal without much success. Antidepressants can help addicts cope with the depression that occurs during acute withdrawal from methamphetamine, but none have been effective in alleviating users' cravings. Benzodiazepines (Valium, Xanax, Librium, etc.) are often prescribed to reduce the anxiety caused by withdrawal, and some patients can get relief from antipsychotic drugs like Thioridazine, haloperidol (brand name Haldol), and olanzapine (brand name Zyprexa), all of which can have a sedating effect.

The Official Patient's Sourcebook on Methamphetamine Dependence paints a disheartening picture of the prospects for pharmacotherapy: "There are currently no particular pharmacological treatments for dependence on amphetamine or amphetamine-like drugs such as methamphetamine. The current pharmacological approach is borrowed from experience with treatment of cocaine dependence. Unfortunately, this approach has not met with much success since no single agent [drug] has proven efficacious in controlled clinical studies."

Withstanding Withdrawal

Many drug treatment providers believe that crystal is the hardest addiction to treat—largely because abusers are often overly excitable and extremely resistant to any form of intervention once the acute effects of methamphetamine use have dissipated.

According to the article "Treatment for Stimulant Use Disorders: Methamphetamine and Cocaine," which was published in 1999 by the SAMHSA Center for Substance Abuse Treatment, a division of the U.S. Department of Health and Human Services, "The initial period of stimulant abstinence is characterized by symptoms of depression, difficulty concentrating, poor memory, irritability, fatigue, craving for cocaine/methamphetamine, and paranoia, especially among methamphetamine users." The article reports that this period of painful abstinence lasts three to five days for cocaine users and 10 to 15 days for methamphetamine users.

Acute withdrawal doesn't last long, although some of the symptoms, like extreme irritability, loss of energy, depression, fearfulness, hyperventilation, and increased appetite can last six to eight months for the occasional crystal user and two to three *years* for longtime users.

CrystalRecovery.com cites a 1996 study, which found that neurological impairment after cessation of drug use can last up to two years. In the worst-case scenario, some addicts never recover and remain mired in a permanent funk due to irreversible brain damage caused by crystal.

Even after the period of acute withdrawal ends, recovering addicts may continue to experience depression, fuzzy-headedness, and anhedonia.

Treating the Symptoms

Meanwhile, UCLA researchers are close to completing a massive five-year study that began in February 2000 and will test the efficacy of another antidepressant, bupropion (brand name Wellbutrin), in treating methamphetamine addiction. The study is being conducted in six cities that are epicenters of crystal use in the United States: San Diego; Honolulu; Kansas City, Missouri; Costa Mesa, California; and Des Moines, Iowa. All subjects are also receiving 90-minute cognitive behavioral therapy sessions three times a week, based on earlier studies that have found pharmacotherapy or cognitive behavioral therapy alone to not be as effective as treatment that combines the two.

Many psychologists believe that the most effective treatment for meth addiction is cognitive behavioral therapy, a school of psychology that focuses on the symptoms (in this case, crystal use) rather than taking a Freudian or psychodynamic approach that delves into a patient's childhood to identify the source of the adult's problems. CrystalRecovery.com states the case for behavioral therapy well: "At this time, the most effective treatment for methamphetamine addiction is cognitive behavioral interventions, which are designed to help modify the patients' thinking, expectations, and behaviors and to increase skills in coping with various life stressors."

UCLA psychiatrist Thomas Newton agrees with CrystalRecovery.com and says, "No medication [for treating crystal addiction] has been shown to be effective. We're actively researching [drug therapy for crystal addiction] right now. The gold standard remains cognitive behavioral group therapy, 90 minutes, three times a week."

In group therapy, Newton says, clients learn how drugs

affect them, which he believes makes relapse less likely. "There are a lot of skills you have to learn not to relapse," he says. Unfortunately, it seems that not many crystal users are able to learn those skills. Newton says cognitive behavioral therapy only has a 10% success rate, which he concedes is "horrible."

The Center for Substance Abuse Treatment takes a cognitive behavioral therapy approach to methamphetamine addiction that includes methods such as "network therapy, in which clients...develop a network of stable, non–substance-abusing support persons." Clients are required to follow through on "plans to break contacts with dealers and other stimulant users and to avoid high-risk places that are strongly associated with stimulant use." Clients are taught how to identify triggers for drug use—and sexual compulsiveness—and to develop ways of combating them. Whenever possible, family members are encouraged to participate in the recovery process, which should also include social support systems such 12-step programs.

Drug testing by urinalysis should be mandatory during treatment. Testing every three to four days is what the Center for Substance Abuse Treatment recommends, along with daily psychotherapy sessions to reinforce drug abstinence and to create a "therapeutic alliance" between the addict and the psychotherapist.

Sometimes cognitive behavioral therapy isn't enough. In such cases, the Center recommends treatment with benzodiazepines such as lorazepam (brand name Ativan) or diazepam (brand name Valium) in order to calm anxious or agitated clients who exhibit symptoms of paranoia and psychosis.

As for clients who become suicidal during withdrawal,

the Center suggests they be treated with the antidepressant trazodone (brand name Desyrel) and the antihistamine diphenhydramine (brand name Benadryl). It should be noted, however, the FDA has posted warnings about the interaction of trazodone with some anti-AIDS medications.

Unlike 12-step programs, which require regular attendance at meetings where participants have been known to describe drug and alcohol use in graphic terms, the Center for Substance Abuse Treatment discourages environments where the recovering addict is repeatedly exposed to "war stories that include euphoric recall." Such story-swapping can trigger relapses and do more harm than good.

Fair Warning

Anyone with an addict's best interests at heart will be careful to avoid setting off his or her triggers. Unfortunately, it's difficult to know what those might be. The 2001 NIDA study, which attempted to identify what triggers sober users to relapse, was only able to come up with the following: "Differences in use patterns indicate different triggers and different times and places when the recovering abuser is particularly vulnerable." Not very helpful.

CrystalRecovery.com, in an attempt to be bit more user-friendly, issues this warning on its home page: "Please note: This Web site contains pictures of methamphetamine, crystal meth, crank, ice...and drug paraphernalia. Do not look at the pictures if they're going to trigger cravings. It's not worth it!"

Many of the addicts interviewed for this book spoke of what would trigger their own drug use. Andrew, the 38-year-old writer, abstained from sex for seven months, fearing that it would trigger the desire to use crystal. Laguna

Beach masseur and bartender Jonathan so vividly described the method of hot-railing that it triggered his desire to use and he terminated his interview soon after he brought up the subject.

Hector—whose dangerous encounter with the racist at the Coral Sands made him finally hit bottom—went to Crystal Meth Anonymous for help. As noted earlier, CMA just made Hector's addiction worse. "CMA meetings did not help. I found that when members of the group shared about their experiences with crystal, the sex talk was 'triggerish.'" And simply talking about his drug use made Hector uncomfortable—not because of the seamy nature of his experiences with the drug but because the conversation made him want to use again, even though he'd managed to accumulate nine months of continuous sobriety.

The Center for Substance Abuse Treatment promotes a more scientific approach to controlling relapses: functional analysis, which the Center describes as teaching clients to identify the triggers that cause relapse and encouraging them to identify the short-term and long-term effects of their drug use.

Clients also learn relapse-prevention techniques, which include short-circuiting the relapse process by identifying high-risk environments and warning signs of relapse, developing coping mechanisms and stress-reduction skills, "enhancing self-efficacy in dealing with potential relapse situations," engaging in healthful leisure programs, quickly identifying slips before they turn into "full-blown relapse," and accepting responsibility for slips.

But the Center for Substance Abuse Treatment agrees with the 12-step belief that relapse is part of recovery: "Early slips should not be considered tragic failures but rather simple mistakes." In anticipation of relapses, addicts are required to draw up verbal contracts with their treatment counselors in which they promise to remain clean and sober for a specific and short period of time.

Tough Love

The Center for Substance Abuse Treatment does not subscribe to the 12-step tenet of "tough love," which can take the form of badgering by other patients and even drug counselors, whom the Center says should be "warm, friendly, engaging, empathetic, straightforward, and nonjudgmental." The Center cites a practical rather than theoretical reason for not taking a tough love approach to treating the addict: "Authoritarian and confrontational behavior by the staff can substantially increase the potential for violence."

But drug counselor Cory Quashen disagrees, advocating what some might see as a "tough love treatment." "Major withdrawal from crystal is emotional, not so much physical," Quashen says. To treat the physical addiction, he explains, "we throw somebody in the closet for three days and give him medication," usually a sedative like Ativan, to alleviate the symptoms of withdrawal. "Three days later, the physical addiction is gone, but then they have to deal with the psychological addiction. There's not much physical addiction coming off the drug, but it's one of the most emotionally addictive drugs there are."

How to Help

To help drug counselors and friends and family of the drug addict recognize the symptoms of chronic crystal use, the Center for Substance Abuse Treatment has identified these signs of drug abuse: nasal perforations and nose bleeds from snorting crystal; missing and/or rotting teeth; bleeding and infected gums; muscle cramping caused by dehydration; dermatitis (reddening of the skin) around the mouth from smoking crystal; the smell of stale urine caused by anhydrous ammonia used to manufacture crystal; skin lesions; and severe constipation caused by dehydration and lack of fiber in the diet.

The Center offers an encyclopedic list of the physiological effects of long-term crystal addiction: extreme fatigue caused by insomnia; dramatic weight loss; anemia; anorexia; cachexia (wasting syndrome); poor hygiene; skin disorders such as itching, hives, pruritus (itchiness), and urticaria (hypersensitivity to heat); hair loss; muscle pain and tenderness; heart damage caused by the contamination of drugs with other ingredients used in the manufacturing process; hypertension (high blood pressure); kidney and liver damage; difficulty breathing; pulmonary edema (swelling of the lungs); headaches; strokes; seizures; blindness; choreoathetoid disorder (involuntary movement); sexual dysfunction; cerebral hemorrhages; cognitive impairment; and bowel and gastrointestinal problems.

The Center's list of common psychological and behavioral effects of long-term crystal use is also extensive: paranoia with "misinterpretation of environmental cues," psychoses and delusions, suicidal ideation, acute anxiety, eating disorders, and apprehensiveness accompanied by a sense of hopelessness and impending doom that often resembles a panic attack.

Many drug users are cross-addicted, which means they're addicted to more than one drug. The Center urges clients and their loved ones to recognize the connection between methamphetamine use and other drug use.

"Clients should be encouraged to throw out substance-related items," the Center says, recommending that family members and sober friends help the addict dispose of the other drugs besides methamphetamine.

The Center warns its drug counselors to be prepared for the paranoia-induced violence that often accompanies long-term crystal use. Drug counselors are urged to keep the patient in touch with reality by using the client's name frequently and by identifying themselves as counselors who want to help the patient. Therapy sessions should take place in a calm, soothing environment in rooms large enough that the patient does not feel claustrophobic or trapped. Claustrophobia can also be countered by keeping the patient close to the door, but the Center warns that the counselor should never let the patient get between him and the door, thus cutting off the counselor's means of escape if the patient becomes violent. A violent patient can often be calmed by the counselor's empathetic reassurance that he realizes how much distress the patient feels.

Violence during withdrawal from crystal is apparently so common that the Center warns counselors to remove objects from the room that could be turned into weapons. Counselors should also check to see if the patient is carrying weapons. The potential for violence is so great that the Center says, "Be prepared to show force if necessary by having a backup plan for help and having chemical and physical restraints immediately available."

Since it's expected that many patients will relapse, part of the treatment for intravenous crystal users should include lessons in HIV prevention, including disinfecting needles with chlorine bleach. The Center also recommends the controversial practice of needle-exchange programs to halt the spread of HIV and AIDS. To cope with life after meth, patients should receive job training. The Center says that there's a need for more drug counselors in prisons because the violent behavior of crystal users often lands them behind bars.

Jay's Way

Jay, the Webmaster of QuitMeth.com, strongly disagrees with the claim made by *The Official Patient's Sourcebook on Methamphetamine Dependence* that there are currently no pharmacological treatments for dependence on methamphetamine. And he doesn't feel the hands-on treatment of crystal users practiced by the Center for Substance Abuse Treatment is necessary.

In a world where instant gratification takes too long, QuitMeth.com is a mail-order treatment program that has only three steps instead of 12 and promises clients that they will be free of methamphetamine cravings within 14 days. Jay writes, "At QuitMeth.com, we believe that the initial detox period is 14 days before you can really say that you're clean. Then we can work on how you're going to stay clean and enjoy a richer and more rewarding life."

QuitMeth.com's program has two phases: In Phase One, the client receives over-the-counter drugs and vitamins to ease withdrawal symptoms. In Phase Two, the client deals with the psychological component of addiction. "We address the triggers in your mind that can cause you to relapse after you have been clean for some time."

The three steps in the addiction recovery program Jay has created are (1) say goodbye, (2) quit, and (3) give back. "With the QuitMeth.com program, we teach you how to say goodbye, how to quit, and how to pay restitution for your soul by giving back to the world what you have taken away. This is a full-service program that helps you in the end to forgive yourself and relieve all your feelings of guilt."

Since crystal use often devastates the user financially, as well as psychologically and physically, QuitMeth.com helps the recovering addict get back on his feet economically too—with a free audiotape that shows clients how to sell products on eBay. "Get back on your feet. Put some extra money in your pocket. Start enjoying your new freedom. The audiotape, 'How to sell stuff on eBay' is my gift to you to help you get your life back," Jay says.

Compared to the cost of inpatient rehab programs, QuitMeth.com is cheap at $300 for the videotape, audiotapes, over-the-counter drugs, and vitamins that are part of the program's treatment. "It's $300 because it works. It's $300 because it's worth it, and it's $300 because if it were free, you wouldn't watch the video, you wouldn't listen to the tapes, and [the treatment program] wouldn't work."

The most eye-catching item on QuitMeth.com's Web site is its heretical notion that drug addiction doesn't fit the disease model. "Cancer is a disease. Diabetes is a disease. Alzheimer's is a disease. Drug addiction isn't a disease." QuitMeth.com believes it's a "slap in the face" to anyone suffering from a "real" disease to call drug addiction a disease too; plus, the disease allows addicts to avoid responsibility for ending their drug use. "Do we really need any more excuses to be drug addicts?" the Web site asks.

QuitMeth.com also dismisses the 12-step belief that relapse is part of recovery. That philosophy gives the drug user an excuse to relapse and lets pricey rehab programs justify their high failure rates, according to QuitMeth.com.

"If you plant it in someone's head that relapse is expected, then you're damning that person's future. Statements like [relapse is part of recovery] are built-in excuses for the failures of drug treatment centers. How else can you justify spending upwards of $10,000 only to have the program fail? Giving you the option to slip is giving you yet another reason to be a drug addict."

Life After Meth

Even though Sam is over the acute withdrawal phase, he seems to be one of the many crystal users who remain miserable even after their drug use has ended. Sam got clean and sober at age 19 after using crystal since the age of 14. During that five-year period, he binged on crystal daily, usually snorting or smoking but sometimes injecting the drug. Some of his binges lasted six days with no sleep.

Sam overdosed twice and ended up in the emergency room, where he was prescribed a benzodiazepine to sedate him and the antidepressant paroxetine (brand name Paxil). Sam stopped using for a while, but then went on another binge that lasted two days and sent him back to the E.R., where he says, "I cried the entire time, mainly because I wanted to quit so badly and was miserable."

In a feckless attempt to get clean and sober, Sam decided to do what is known in 12-step programs as "pulling a geographic" and moved from Ohio to Baltimore to get away from his drug connections. "I had to relocate from Ohio because the drug is such a problem there," he says. But he soon found a drug source in Baltimore. Based on his posted message on the Koch Web site, Sam seems like one of those lost souls who remain in despair even after getting clean and sober: "I was so used to speeding and wrapped up in the feeling of complete control and euphoria that my brain is now wired for good."

The main symptom Sam suffers from is anxiety, although based on his description of the way he feels after stopping drugs, it may be more likely that he is having panic attacks. "I have enough anxiety every day for 20 people," he says. Sam's anxiety manifests itself in heart palpitations, and he also experiences numbness in his left arm, which can be signal an incipient heart attack. One of the many things that make him anxious is the fear that he's going to die of a heart attack any minute.

Sam's teeth are also falling out, due to a deficiency in calcium caused by the drug and poor diet. Sam's other symptoms include shortness of breath and joint pain from hyperextending his arm when it begins to go numb. With great understatement, he writes, "As you can see, my long-term use of meth has left me in a sticky situation. I would trade any body part for the anxiety to go away for good." He cries "all the time" because he feels as though he is "missing out on my entire life because the only thing I can stay focused on is my anxiety."

Sam feels good every morning when he first wakes up, but after a short while the anxiety attacks begin. For the rest of the day, the only thing he can concentrate on is his violently beating heart. "It's not a normal anxiety problem, because it takes me to the point that I want to die because I just can't for one minute relax and take deep breaths."

Sam's message to others still using crystal isn't an optimistic one. He is hardly an exemplar for better living through sobriety. "To the people who are still using meth or thinking about trying it, I can only tell you that you will not be happy with the way you feel after you're done…if you're not dead by that time."

Web of Destruction

Yahoo hosts several meth groups, including one for IV-crystal users called methrecovery@yahoogroups.com, which is, according to Yahoo, "devoted to people who slam [inject] crystal," and features this chirpy welcome to newcomers from the page's Webmaster: "Hello, fellow tweakers and tweakettes. I have built a site where hopefully some of you will share your stories and post pics. Crystal is a common drug; it deserves a club. I'm not here to encourage or discourage use, only to create a nonjudgmental place for us to gather, especially slammers." The Webmaster adds that the site features "stories and pics of people who shoot crystal meth."

In response to a request to interview drug users for this book, many members of the Crystal Meth Slammers Web sent me enraged e-mails. One active crystal user wrote, "How dare you bother poor gay guys you're trying to turn into research subjects!" The common thread among all the angry e-mails was the paranoia typical of crystal users who often take offense at imagined insults while tweaking.

An AOL subscriber named Kitty responded to my initial request for an interview with a vitriolic note that was most notable for its defensiveness. The Oceanside, California, resident, sent this livid e-mail: "Dude, I am a 20-year veteran of this arena. I have a college degree, a family, friends, a home on the beach, I don't have to work, I use on a daily basis, it's my choice. You have no idea who you're talking to. And you're stereotyping, just horribly. I should write a book about how you should not be allowed to write books with your myopic views and closed mind."

In her autobiographical profile on AOL, Kitty says,

"Mostly I love my awesome son...and being high a lot." This daily consumer of crystal also offers some scary information about her occupation: "I am a medical assistant, when I work..." Kitty's occupation is especially disturbing since it supports a claim made by Bob, the nurse who confessed that he and other crystal-impaired nurses he knows have made so many medication errors that they ended up killing patients.

The Southern California treatment center Solutions for Recovery suggests that the angry responses from crystal users solicited as interview subjects are typical. The clinic's Web page says, "In fact, after a while, a heavy methamphetamine user will actually resent people, places and activities not able to fit in with methamphetamine use."

To its credit, Yahoo also offers a Web site called MethRecovery, which attracts people who aren't in denial about the problems crystal has caused them.

Pro-drug Web sites often have the quality of a carnival fun-house mirror. They reflect the values and concerns espoused by antidrug sites but in a distorted, mirthful way. One pro-crystal site offers a diagnostic questionnaire entitled, "How to Tell You're a Junkie." The "test," which follows, satirizes the signs of crystal addiction, such as paranoia and drug craving.

You're a Junkie If...
❑ You scored some shit from a "last resort" connection and it seems to turn into a green gel when you try to smoke it.
❑ Everybody you know suddenly becomes a cop.
❑ You're selling food stamps for 1/2 value to get off.
❑ You're up for a week one day.
❑ You go BACK to the loser that sold you the green dope to try and cop more.

❏ You're hanging around with people you can't stand—
[whom] you'd snub on the street—just to get a fix.

❏ 57 projects suddenly come to a screeching halt due to
lack of floor space...and you can't remember what the
hell the point of any of them were.

❏ You're riding your bike (with no light) at 2 A.M. with no
shirt on in the middle of January eating a Popsicle...
SWEATING like a motherfucker and wondering WHY the
cops pulled your spun ass over."

Gallows humor from the damned.

-13-
Getting Over Tina

"WHAT GOT ME THROUGH THE FIRST YEAR OF SOBRIETY WAS THE FEAR OF GOING BACK TO JAIL."

—RICHARD

"I'M VERY LUCKY I'VE NEVER RELAPSED."

—JULES

"I INJECTED [CRYSTAL], ATE IT, SNORTED IT, DRANK IT. I SOLD IT AND I MADE IT.... I SKIPPED OUT ON $5,000 BAIL.... THEN I MADE THE DECISION THAT I HAD TO START MY LIFE OVER AGAIN."

—DAVID BOUCHARD

You may be reading this book because you suspect that you have a problem with your use of methamphetamine. In his book *Ties That Bind,* psychologist Guy Baldwin offers the following checklist of items that, if familiar, probably indicate you have a problem with crystal:

❏ Legal troubles arise, including arrest.
❏ Financial outlay for crystal has become significant and includes a "drug budget."
❏ A potential sex partner may reject you because you're unwilling to have sex without crystal.
❏ Friends begin to worry about you.
❏ You start missing too many Mondays at work, and sometimes Tuesdays as well.
❏ Health may deteriorate.
❏ You get uptight when you can't score drugs.

"If you suspect you have a problem," Baldwin suggests, "you might consciously examine the cost-benefit ratio of drug-taking to see if you have become an abuser." The psychologist departs from substance abuse orthodoxy when he offers the hope that chronic users can heal themselves without professional or peer-group intervention. "If you're worried enough about yourself," Baldwin says, "you may be able to quit all by yourself. But if you keep slipping back into old, worrisome behavior, you might consider a recovery program or a therapist. And if you do neither, your life is probably in danger and perhaps the lives of others as well."

A large amount of Baldwin's practice is devoted to drug addicts, and many of his patients have told him, "It's my life, and I can do whatever I choose to do with it. And it's none of your business." To these sorts of comments, Baldwin responds, "Caution is in order here, because the right to experiment with drugs is also the right to destroy yourself."

(See page 246 and 247 for two more tests to determine whether you have a crystal addiction.)

Doing Time With Robert Downey

Television actor Richard believes trouble with the law scared him straight. When crystal made him too agitated and paranoid, Richard would drink to excess in bars to cushion the crash. After three DUIs, he was sentenced to three months in the Los Angeles County Jail. His cell mate during part of his incarceration was the actor Robert Downey, Jr. Both men were kept isolated from the rest of the prison population because they were targets for other inmates who wanted to make a name for themselves by assaulting or even killing a celebrity.

Richard ended up serving only 17 days of his three-month sentence. Ironically, it was *after* he got out that he hit bottom. Shortly before his release from jail, a guard told Richard that they had lost his clothes, and Richard was ordered to pick out a new wardrobe from what had been left behind by former inmates. This was the beginning of Richard's bottom. "The underwear was stained...disgusting!" he says, recoiling at the memory. The secondhand shoes he chose curled up at the toes because they were so old.

"I looked like a bum," Richard says. But his thoughts after his release at 2 in the morning (the time chosen because most bars close then) were not on the fashion disaster he had become, but where he could score what he promised himself would be one last binge on crystal.

First, however, Richard had to return to his home in Van Nuys, an outlying L.A. district in the San Fernando Valley 18 miles from downtown, where the County Jail is located. Somehow he managed to find a cab in the ghost town downtown L.A. becomes after business hours. Once he got in the cab he asked the driver how much it would cost to go to Van Nuys. The cabdriver said, "Forty dollars...but I want you to show it to me."

"He wanted me to show him the money," Richard says.

That was the moment when the actor hit bottom. Richard looked like a bum in his soiled clothes, and a cab driver thought he was such a lowlife that he couldn't afford to pay for cab fare. At the time, Richard was a recurring character on an Emmy-winning sitcom and somewhat of a celebrity. But at this moment, "I was just a bum on Bauchet Street" near the County Jail. "That's when I hit bottom—being mistaken for a homeless person. With an ego like mine, it made me hit bottom."

That was six years ago, and Richard hasn't relapsed since. Whenever he feels the urge to use again, he plays in his mind the "tape" of himself looking like riff raff and being insulted by a cabdriver. His sobriety is further strengthened by the warning he received from the judge who sentenced him to jail. "I haven't used since December 11, 1997. No relapses. What got me through the first year of sobriety was the fear of going back to jail. The judge said that if I got another DUI, he would put me in jail for a year and 20 days," Richard says.

On one occasion, Richard did attempt a relapse, but the results were comical rather than disastrous. The actor planned to spend the Christmas holidays with his difficult family after getting out of jail. He told himself that he needed crystal to steel himself for a prickly family reunion, plus during the holidays there were no acting auditions, so Richard could binge during the break.

Richard went to a bar frequented by male prostitutes in West Hollywood and found a young hustler willing to introduce him to a drug dealer. They took a cab to a dangerous section of downtown L.A., where the prostitute disappeared for a bit, then returned with what he insisted was crystal but which Richard was certain was drywall. Richard was so desperate to get high, however, that he returned home with the drywall and ground it into a powder. "I inhaled drywall! For weeks afterwards, whenever I coughed, I coughed up pieces of drywall."

Richard's experience with counterfeit crystal was not unique. With the proliferation of meth-making labs, the purity of crystal has steadily decreased in proportion to the greed of the manufacturer. Lab tests of alleged methamphetamine seized by Dallas police in 2001 revealed that one fourth of the impounded substance was actually derived from crushed Sheetrock, a form of drywall. The Dallas police also reported that fully half of all the cocaine they had seized that year was cut with crushed Sheetrock. DEA Chief of Operations Rogelio Guevara told a House subcommittee in 2003, "The average purity of methamphetamine seized by the DEA has declined significantly from 71.9% in 1994 to 44% in 2002." Unknowingly, crystal users are smoking and injecting more filler ingredients as the drug is "stepped on" to increase the amount available for sale.

Richard's sponsor insisted that the drywall incident qualified as a "slip" or relapse, but Richard disagreed. "I said it wasn't a slip because I didn't get high. It was drywall, after all."

First Time's a Charm: A Rare Success Story

Jules, 37, had been snorting crystal daily for five years and was unemployed, broke, and nearing homelessness when he pulled a geographic moved from Chicago to Fresno, California, to get away from the drug scene. "One day I just got on a plane and never looked back," he says.

Jules is an exception to the rule that relocating doesn't work, because the addict will soon find a new source of drugs in his new place of residence—although Jules did more than pull a geographic. A few months after moving to Fresno, he began attending 12-step meetings. That was nine years ago, and Jules hasn't slipped since then—making him also an exception to the "third time's a charm" of recovery-relapse parlance.

Today, the former bartender with no ambition is a corporate attorney and litigator who hopes in a few years to become an assistant district attorney. "Crystal stymied me career-wise. I never tried to accomplish anything professionally [while using]...and I never would have even dreamed about going to law school," Jules says.

At his bartending job, the handsome Jules got almost all his drugs for free from patrons besotted with his movie-star looks. His drug of choice, he jokes, was "more." Six months before moving to Fresno, he quit his job as a bartender, a decision he calls "an act of grace" because it cut off his supply of free drugs. Suddenly, Jules realized he was unemployable and "pretty much on my way to living on the street. My life simply became one miserable experience after another. I can't really explain why I hit bottom. I just got tired of the whole scene."

During drug runs, Jules barely ate or drank. "I was just wasting away. Once in a while I'd eat a doughnut," Jules says. He also found himself hanging out with too many "dangerous people carrying guns," including his drug dealer. And Jules didn't even enjoy sex on crystal. "Everything fell by the wayside—friends, family, even sex," he says.

His first 12-step meeting was "miraculous," he says, because it completely lifted his obsession to use drugs, which he says has never returned. "I'm very lucky I've never relapsed," Jules says. And although sometimes he toys with having a drink socially, Jules has never acted on that impulse because he fears alcohol would eventually lead him back to drugs.

Starting Over

Legal and medical problems scared David Bouchard straight. "I injected [crystal], ate it, snorted it, drank it. I sold it and I made it," he says. Two things finally made him realize he had a problem with drugs: "Legal stuff and having seizures on the street and having to be taken to the hospital in an ambulance." His legal problems were mostly a case of "being in the wrong place at the wrong time." David was arrested four times for possession and spent six months in the L.A. County Jail after he failed to show up in court because he was too high on crystal to function.

David compounded his legal problems by jumping a $5,000 bail bond. "My best thinking while stoned was to change my name," he quips, because with a new identity he could have tried to skirt his legal difficulties. He then hid out for eight months in a residential treatment center. "Then I made the decision that I had to start my life over again." By June 2004, David had accumulated six years of continuous sobriety.

It's Our Problem

The National Institute on Drug Abuse offers a disturbing list of other problems associated with methamphetamine use: automobile accidents; explosions and fires triggered by the illegal manufacture of methamphetamine; environmental contamination; increased criminal activity, including domestic violence; emergency room and other medical costs; the spread of infectious diseases, including HIV, AIDS and hepatitis; and lost worker productivity.

While many addicts claim it's no one else's business if they use crystal, society picks up part of the tab for substance abuse. As NIDA has observed, "Economic costs also fall on governments, which must allocate additional resources for social services and law enforcement."

For concerned friends and loved ones of meth users, here's one last plea: To determine if someone you know is

abusing this vicious drug, please read the following
checklist of methamphetamine use symptoms provided
by the Substance Abuse and Mental Health Services
Administration (SAMHSA), an agency of the U.S.
Department of Health and Human Services.

❑ Inability to sleep
❑ Increased sensitivity to noise
❑ Nervous physical activity, like scratching
❑ Irritability, dizziness, or confusion
❑ Extreme anorexia (loss of body weight)
❑ Tremors or convulsions
❑ Increased heart rate and blood pressure
❑ The presence of paraphernalia for snorting crystal,
    such as razor blades, mirrors, and straws
❑ The presence of IV paraphernalia, such as syringes,
    heated spoons, or surgical tubing.

If you suspect someone you know or love has a problem
with methamphetamine use, SAMHSA advises, "Be a real
friend. Encourage your friend to stop [using meth] or seek
professional help. You might even save a life."

Resources

Counselors

Edwin Bayrd, executive director of the UCLA AIDS Institute and an expert on HIV transmission due to illicit drug use, can be contacted at HIV Newsline.com.

Michael Majeski, a drug abuse specialist who works with gay and lesbian youth, can be e-mailed at drmichaelm@glassla.org.

To speak to a counselor at Solutions for Recovery, a drug treatment facility in Dana Point, California, phone (800) 868-8514.

Legal Information

For more information on the criminal penalties associated with methamphetamine use, call the National Institute of Justice's National Criminal Justice Reference Service at (800) 851-3420 or (301) 519-5500 or access its Web site at www.ojp.usdoj.gov/nij. For a free, immediate consultation with an attorney, access www.thebestdefense.com.

Rehab Facilities and Information

Treatment Information

For information about using cognitive behavioral therapy to treat methamphetamine addiction, call the National Institute on Drug Abuse at (301) 443-6173 or access the topic online at www.nida.nih.gov/TXManuals/CBT/CBT1.htm. For information on accessing and financing drug treatment and rehabilitation, call (301) 443-4060. For general inquiries, call the NIDA Public Information Office at (301) 443-1124.

For information on clinical trials to test the efficacy of the drug ondansetron (brand name Zofran) to treat methamphetamine withdrawal, call the Southwest Texas Addiction Research & Technology Center at (210) 562-5400.

For comprehensive information about methamphetamine abuse and other meth-related issues, call the National Clearinghouse for Alcohol and Drug Information (NCADI) at (800) 729-6686 or access its Web site at www.health.org.

Treatment Centers and Support groups

Addiction Resource Center: (800) 390-4056.

The Behavioral Health Services Hollywood Recovery Center offers outpatient treatment for drug and alcohol addiction: (323) 461-3161.

Being Alive in West Hollywood, California, hosts Crystal Meth Anonymous meetings: (310) 289-2551.

Callen-Lorde Community Health Center, New York City: (212) 271-7200.

C.A.R.E., or Comprehensive Addiction Rehabilitation Education Inc., has developed a treatment program that blends Eastern and alternative medicine with Western technology. The C.A.R.E. inpatient center is located in a beautiful vacation setting: (866) 494-0866.

Gay and Lesbian Adolescent Social Services (GLASS) in West Hollywood offers group therapy for methamphetamine addiction. Call (310) 358-872or contact counselor Orlando Rivera at OrlandoR@glassla.org.

Gay Men's Health Crisis, New York City: (212) 367-1000; Hotline: (212) 807-6655.

Giordano and Goldfarb Holistic Addiction Treatment Center, Inc.: (800) 559-9503.

The Lesbian, Gay, Bisexual & Transgender Community Center, New York City: (212) 620-7310.

The Los Angeles Gay & Lesbian Center offers group therapy for methamphetamine addiction: (323) 464-1319.

Narconon International
(800) 722-5570, www.narconon.org.

Solutions for Recovery, in Dana Point, California, offers a comprehensive inpatient program: (800) 784-4791, www.solutions4recovery.com.

The Sunshine Coast Health Centre in Powell River, British Columbia, Canada, offers residential alcohol and drug treatment programs:
(866) 487-9010; www.sunshinecoasthealthcentre.ca.

The Tarzana Treatment Center in Los Angeles's western San Fernando Valley offers inpatient treatment for methamphetamine addiction: (818) 996-1051.

Transitions of America in Delray Beach, Florida, offers both inpatient and outpatient methamphetamine treatment programs: (866) 732-4055; www.toa-addictions.com.

The Van Ness Recovery House in the Hollywood district of Los Angeles offers inpatient treatment for drug and alcohol addiction: (323) 463-4266.

Treatment Referrals

Center for Substance Abuse Treatment (CSAT) 24-hour hotline for drug treatment referrals: (800) 662-HELP.

SAMHSA state-by-state map for locating inpatient and outpatient drug and alcohol abuse treatment facilities: http://findtreatment.samhsa.gov/facilitylocator.htm.

Online Resources

AIDSHotline.org: California's HIV/STD Referral Database

AIDSMEDS.com

Anti-Meth.com: An excellent home page–style site with a chat board and many resource links.

ClubDrugs.org

CrystalRecovery.com

DanceSafe.org

KCI.org (formerly the Koch Crime Institute)

LifeorMeth.com

MethAbuse.net

National Institute on Drug Abuse resources:
Articles are also available by calling (888) 644-6432.

> InfoFacts on Methamphetamine
> http://www.nida.nih.gov/infofax/methamphetamine.html
>
> Methamphetamine Abuse and Addiction:
> National Institute on Drug Abuse Report Series
> http://165.112.78.61/ResearchReports/methamph/
> methamph.html
>
> NIDA Notes (online drug abuse journal)
> www.drugabuse.gov/NIDA_Notes/NNIndex.html

New York Crystal Meth Anonymous: nycma.org

QuitMeth.com

Tweaker.org

WebMD.com

Yahoo Groups: Meth Recovery:
   http: health.groups.yahoo.com/group/methrecovery/

For eye-opening stories about crystal abuse that may scare potential users straight, access the Meth Monster link at QuitMeth.com or the True Stories section of Tweaker.org.

STDs

Chlamydia

Chlamydia infects three million Americans every year, and it's the most common bacterial STD in the United States. Epidemiologists say chlamydia is twice as common as gonorrhea, six times as common as genital herpes, and 30 times as common as syphilis. Chlamydia is caused by the microbe *Chlamydia trachomatis,* which has both viral and bacterial properties. Anal or vaginal sex is the main route of transmission. If someone who has chlamydia touches his eyes, an inflammation of membranes in the eye, known as conjunctivitis, can result.

Although chlamydia is easily cured with antibiotics, those who have the disease often remain asymptomatic and unaware that they're infected. Of the total number of women infected with chlamydia, approximately 75% don't realize they're infected until they suffer severe complications such as damage to the fallopian tubes, which causes pelvic inflammatory disease and can lead to sterility. Half a million women become infected with chlamydia every year.

Fifty percent of men remain asymptomatic once they've been infected with chlamydia. When left untreated, chlamydia in men can lead to epididymitis, an inflammatory disease that causes painful swelling of the testicles, urethra, and scrotum. Epididymitis can also cause sterility.

Syphilis

The bacterium *Treponema pallidum* causes syphilis, which is mostly spread through sexual contact, but can also be contracted through bodily fluids. Syphilis responds to antibiotics, but its symptoms mimic other diseases, and the infected individual may be unaware that he or she has the disease.

There are four stages in the progression of syphilis. In the primary stage, a painless sore or chancre appears. The sore is often found in the genital area, the anus, the mouth, or anywhere else the bacteria has entered the body.

In the secondary stage, a skin rash appears four to 10 weeks after the primary-stage chancre surfaces. Secondary syphilis is much more contagious than primary syphilis, and the second stage can enter any mucous membrane in the body.

The third stage is called the latent stage because the patient still remains asymptomatic. The fourth is the killer stage. If syphilis is left untreated at this stage, it can cause heart problems, mental illness, blindness, and various neurological problems. At the fourth stage, the patient can survive if treated with antibiotics. But antibiotics cannot reverse damage done to the body during the earlier stages of the disease.

Despite antibiotics, syphilis remains one of the most common diseases in the United States. In 1999, the Centers for Disease Control and Prevention began a campaign to combat syphilis, with a goal of lowering the number of reported cases in the United States to 1,000 per year by 2005.

In the general population, syphilis infections continue to decline and are at the lowest levels since the Centers for Disease Control and Prevention began tracking the disease in 1941. However, there has been an increase in the rate of syphilis infections in people who are also infected with HIV. Especially hard hit by the double whammy of syphilis and HIV are gay men, according to

AOL's WebMD. The syphilitic chancre provides an open door for the AIDS virus.

Syphilis has claimed such famous victims as Henry VIII, Al Capone, Randolph Churchill (Winston Churchill's father), the German philosopher Friedrich Nietzsche, and the French author Guy de Maupassant.

Gonorrhea

Like syphilis, gonorrhea is transmitted mainly through sexual contact, but it can also be spread by body fluids. Another similarity to the epidemiology of syphilis is that gonorrhea often appears in people who have sex with a variety of partners.The gonorrhea bacterium, called *Neisseria gonorrhoeae,* flourishes in mucous membranes such as the warm, moist areas of women's reproductive tracts and in the urethra, mouth, throat and anus of both men and women.

With 650,000 known cases every year, gonorrhea is one of the most often-reported diseases in the United States. Gonorrhea is especially prevalent among the young, with 75% of reported cases falling in the age group 15 to 29. The highest infection rate among women occurs between ages 15 to 19; for men, the highest rate occurs between ages 20 to 24.

Gonorrhea is often asymptomatic, or the symptoms are wrongly attributed to other diseases. WebMD provides a list of symptoms that include:

❑ Greenish, yellow, or whitish discharge from the penis
❑ A burning sensation while urinating
❑ A burning sensation in the throat caused by oral sex
❑ Swollen glands caused by oral sex

Men typically become symptomatic two to five days after being exposed to gonorrhea, although it may take up to 30 days for symptoms to appear in some infected individuals.

Gonorrhea responds to both oral and injectable antibiotics. To determine if someone is infected, a sample of fluid is taken from the cervix in women and the urethra and anus in men.

WebMD urges anyone diagnosed with gonorrhea to inform all sex partners they've had within the past three months of possible exposure to the disease. Sex partners may easily remain asymptomatic and therefore unaware they've been infected.

If left untreated due to the absence of symptoms, gonorrhea can cause severe health problems. It damages the prostate gland and causes scarring within the urethra, which makes urination painful. Gonorrhea can spread to the bloodstream and the joints, a development that can be fatal. Individuals with untreated gonorrhea are more susceptible to HIV infection.

WebMD recommends that anyone who experiences a discharge or pain while urinating or develops a sore or rash to abstain from sex and consult with a physician. Recent sex partners should be informed so they can be tested for gonorrhea.

Hepatitis A

Hepatitis A is a viral disease that affects the liver. A healthy liver is important because the organ fights infection, stops bleeding, removes drugs and toxins from the blood, and also stores and provides energy when needed.

Hepatitis A is spread by eating or drinking something that has been handled by someone with feces on his hands, a mode of transmission known as "fecal-oral." Hepatitis A flourishes in places where people neglect personal hygiene.

Most cases of hepatitis A occur among family members or others in close contact with someone else who is infected. Like many diseases, hepatitis A is often asymptomatic. Symptoms, when they do occur, include fever, fatigue, loss of appetite, nausea, abdominal discomfort, dark urine, and jaundice, which turns the skin and eyes yellow. The disease typically goes away after two months, although some cases have been known to last up to six months.

To avoid infection with hepatitis A, the National Institutes of Health advises, "Always wash your hands after using the bathroom, changing a diaper, or before preparing or eating food."

Two vaccines against hepatitis A are available: immune globulin and hepatitis A vaccine. The vaccination protocol consists of two injections given two months apart. Immune globulin contains antibodies against hepatitis A and can be given before or after exposure to the virus. Immune globulin can be effective as long as two weeks after exposure. Hepatitis A vaccine can be given to anyone more than 2 years old, but it must be administered before exposure to the virus. The NIH recommends that the vaccine be used as a prophylactic for people at risk for hepatitis A.

Vaccines currently approved in the United States are sold under the brand names of Havrix and Vaqta. The NIH also recommends vaccination for people who travel to or work in countries with high incidences of hepatitis A. Those at risk include tourists, military personnel, missionaries, and students studying abroad in developing countries where the rate of hepatitis A infection is high. Vaccination should take place four weeks prior to traveling abroad.

Although only 100 people per year die of hepatitis A in the United States, Laurene Mascola, chief of acute communicable disease control for the Los Angeles County Department of Health Services, urges that everyone, not just those at greater risk, get vaccinated. "Why be exposed to a disease for which there's a preventive measure?" Mascola asks. Contracting hepatitis A "is a terrible thing. You can get very sick for a month or two and be off work."

The NIH believes gay men should be vaccinated because they may have weakened immune systems unable to fend off hepatitis A. Gay men who inject drugs are at even greater risk for contracting the disease.

Hepatitis B

An estimated 78,000 Americans are infected with hepatitis B, and 5,000 Americans die of the disease every year. The average American has a one in 20 chances of contracting hepatitis B during his or her lifetime. According to the NIH, risk of infection is higher if an individual:

❏ Has sex with someone infected with hepatitis B
❏ Has sex with more than one partner
❏ Injects drugs
❏ Has male-on-male sex
❏ Lives in the same house with someone who suffers from chronic hepatitis B
❏ Has a job that involves contact with human blood
❏ Is a patient at a home for the developmentally disabled or works there
❏ Has hemophilia
❏ Travels to places where hepatitis is pandemic

If your parents were born in Southeast Asia, Africa, the Amazon basin in South America, the Pacific Islands, or the Middle East, you're at greater risk for contracting hepatitis B, according to the NIH.

Hepatitis B is spread by contact with blood or other bodily fluids from an infected individual. Sharing needles or having sex with someone who is infected are two of the most common ways of transmission. Unlike hepatitis A, hepatitis B isn't spread through casual contact or consumption of contaminated food or water.

Twinrix, a combination of the drugs Havrix and Engerix-B, is a vaccine that confers nearly 100% immunity against both hepatitis A and B in a series of three doses. In clinical trials, 100% of patients had developed immunity to hepatitis A one month after the final dose, and 99.7% had developed immunity to hepatitis B. The vaccine provides lifetime immunity against hepatitis A, but a booster shot against hepatitis B must be given every 10 years.

Interferon has shown some clinical promise in treating hepatitis B, but WebMD only recommends interferon treatment if the patient is at risk for cirrhosis (scarring) of the liver or has already developed it.

Less effective in treating hepatitis B is a drug used to combat AIDS called lamivudine (brand names Combivir and Epivir). Unfortunately, both AIDS patients and those infected with hepatitis B soon develop resistance to lamivudine because of viral mutation. But there's hope. Some drugs that have proven effective against HIV, such as Lobucavir, adefovir (brand name Hepsera), and bisPOC-PMPA, are being studied as treatments for hepatitis B.

Some people who develop hepatitis B never shake the virus and become lifetime carriers of the disease. At least 1 million people in the United States are chronic carriers, and they can infect others. As the NIH has observed: "You may have hepatitis B [and be spreading the disease] and not know it." Although some people with hepatitis B remain asymptomatic, others who contract the disease should be aware of the following symptoms: yellow eyes and/or skin, loss of appetite, nausea, vomiting, fever, stomach or joint pain, and extreme fatigue that prevents the sufferer from working for weeks or months.

Because the vaccines for hepatitis A and B do not confer complete immunity, the NIH stresses the importance of prevention. Currently, there is no complete cure for hepatitis after infection.

Hepatitis C

The symptoms of hepatitis C include fatigue, nausea, fever, loss of appetite, stomach cramps, diarrhea, dark yellow urine, and yellowish eyes and skin. According to the NIH, these are the modes of transmission for viral hepatitis C, which is only spread by contact with the blood of someone infected with the virus:

❑ Sharing needles
❑ Getting pricked with a needle that has infected blood on it (hospital workers especially at risk for this reason)
❑ Getting a tattoo or body piercing with unsterilized, dirty tools
❑ Having sex with an infected person, especially if you or your partner has other STDs

A blood test or liver biopsy can determine if someone is infected with hepatitis C. Infected individuals are treated with two drugs, interferon and ribavirin, which are injected subcutaneously three times a week. Chronic carriers of hepatitis C may eventually suffer liver failure, which requires a liver transplant. The NIH offers these tips to avoid contracting hepatitis C:

❑ Wear gloves if you have to touch anyone's blood.
❑ Don't use an infected person's toothbrush, razor, or anything else that might have blood on it.
❑ If you get a tattoo or body piercing, make sure it's done with clean tools.
❑ If you have multiple sex partners, always use a condom.

The NIH also strongly advises that anyone with hepatitis C should never donate blood or plasma, which can then infect recipients with the virus.

Human Papillomavirus (HPV)

Genital warts are skin lesions that appear in the genital region and can be contracted during sex. They're caused by the human papillomavirus (HPV). The cervix, vagina, vulva, urethra, and anus of women can harbor HPV. The penis, scrotum, urethra, and anus are areas where the virus can flourish in men.

Most infections with HPV are latent, which means the warts aren't visible, and the patient remains asymptomatic. For symptomatic HPV, the incubation period is two to three months, although symptoms may appear many years after infection. Skin lesions that do appear look like miniature bunches of cauliflowerets or flat, white patches that are very hard to see.

Unprotected sex, sex with multiple partners, or sexual contact with someone who has multiple sex partners or is infected with HPV puts the individual at greater risk, as does an immune system weakened by HIV. Also, asymptomatic (but not symptomatic) infection with HPV can cause cell mutations that increase the risk of anal and rectal cancer.

Genital warts usually disappear without treatment, although if they cause cosmetic problems, the patient may want to have the warts removed. "Experts disagree on the medical treatment for genital warts because many go away on their own and because treatment does not eliminate" the underlying infection with HPV, which remains for life, according to the WebMD. Even after the warts disappear on their own or are removed, the individual may still be infected and infectious. Protected sex is recommended, even though condoms aren't 100% effective at halting transmission of the virus.

Do You Have a Problem With Crystal?

Only you can decide if you have a substance abuse problem and whether you want to do something about it. But here are two tests designed to help you take a clear look at your behavior.

Seliger's Test

Years ago Robert V. Seliger, a mid–20th century authority on substance abuse, created a list of 20 questions for diagnosing alcoholism titled "Does Drinking Cause You Problems?" Many substance abuse counselors have used his questions to determine if their clients have become addicted to alcohol. And the same questions work equally well if you rephrase them and substitute "crystal use" for "drinking." Here is Dr. Seliger's modified list:

1) Do you lose time from work due to using crystal?
2) Is using crystal making your home life unhappy?
3) Do you do crystal because you're shy with other people?
4) Is using affecting your reputation?
5) Have you ever felt remorse after using?
6) Have you gotten into financial difficulties as a result of your using?
7) Do you turn to lower companions and an inferior environment when using?
8) Does your using make you careless of your family's welfare?
9) Has your ambition decreased since you started using?
10) Do you crave crystal at a definite time daily?
11) Do you want to use the next morning?
12) Does using cause you to have difficulty sleeping?
13) Has your efficiency decreased since you began using?
14) Is using crystal jeopardizing your job or business?
15) Do you use crystal to escape from worries or troubles?
16) Do you use crystal alone?
17) Have you ever had a complete loss of memory (a blackout) as a result of your using?
18) Has your physician ever treated you for crystal addiction?
19) Do you use crystal to build up your self-confidence?
20) Have you ever been in a hospital or other institution on account of using crystal?

Attempts to score yourself Seliger's test can yield disturbing results. To quote Seliger, substituting "crystal addict" for "alcoholic": "If you have answered yes to any one of the questions, there's a definite warning that you may be [a crystal addict]. If you have answered 'yes' to any two questions, the chances are that you're [a crystal addict]. If you have answered 'yes' to three or more questions, you're definitely [a crystal addict]."

NIAAA Test

The National Institute on Alcohol Abuse and Alcoholism (NIAAA) offers a few more questions to determine if you have a substance abuse problem. Again, "crystal" has been substituted for "drinking":

How can you tell if someone has a [crystal] problem? Answering the following four questions can help you find out if you or a loved one has a [crystal] problem.

☐ Have you ever felt you should cut down on your use of crystal?
☐ Have people annoyed you by criticizing your crystal use?
☐ Have you ever felt bad or guilty about using crystal?
☐ Have you ever snorted, smoked, or injected crystal first thing in the morning to get rid of a hangover?

According to NIAAA, one yes answer indicates a possible problem with crystal. More than one yes answer makes it likely that you do have a problem. And if you answered yes to four or more questions, you should seek treatment immediately.

About the Author

Nationally known author and syndicated columnist Frank Sanello has written 15 critically acclaimed nonfiction history books, including *The Opium Wars: The Addiction of One Empire and the Corruption of Another*; *The Knights Templar: God's Warriors, the Devil's Bankers*; and *To Kill a King: An Encyclopedia of Royal Murders and Assassinations from Ancient Egypt to the Present*.

Sanello is currently writing *Faith and Finance in the Renaissance: The Rise and Ruin of the Fugger Empire*, a centuries-spanning epic about the influential family of bankers and patrons of the arts who were the German equivalent of their contemporaries, the Medici.

A journalist for the past 25 years, Sanello has written articles for *The Washington Post*, the *Los Angeles Times*, the *Chicago Tribune*, *The Boston Globe*, and *The New York Times Syndicate*. Sanello was also formerly the film critic for the *Los Angeles Daily News* and a business reporter for UPI.

The author graduated *cum laude* from the University of Chicago and earned a master's degree from UCLA's film school. He also holds a purple belt in tae kwon do and has volunteered as a martial arts instructor at AIDS Project Los Angeles.

Sanello lives in Los Angeles and can be contacted at fsanello@aol.com.